SCIENCE
FUSion

fusion [FYOO • zhuhn] a combination of two
or more things that releases energy

James 2:10

This **Interactive Student Edition** belongs to

Derek Vook

Teacher/Room

Mrs. Kingsolver

HOLT McDOUGAL

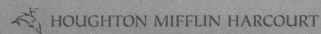

HOUGHTON MIFFLIN HARCOURT

Consulting Authors

Michael A. DiSpezio

Global Educator
North Falmouth, Massachusetts

Michael DiSpezio is a renaissance educator who moved from the research laboratory of a Nobel Prize winner to the K–12 science classroom. He has authored or co-authored numerous textbooks and written more than 25 trade books. For nearly a decade he worked with the JASON Project, under the auspices of the National Geographic Society, where he designed curriculum, wrote lessons, and hosted dozens of studio and location broadcasts. Over the past two decades, he has developed supplementary material for organizations and shows that include PBS *Scientific American Frontiers, Discover* magazine, and the Discovery Channel. He has extended his reach outside the United States and into topics of crucial importance today. To all his projects, he brings his extensive background in science and his expertise in classroom teaching at the elementary, middle, and high school levels.

Marjorie Frank

Science Writer and Content-Area Reading Specialist
Brooklyn, New York

An educator and linguist by training, a writer and poet by nature, Marjorie Frank has authored and designed a generation of instructional materials in all subject areas, including past HMH Science programs. Her other credits include authoring science issues of an award-winning children's magazine; writing game-based digital assessments in math, reading, and language arts; and serving as instructional designer and co-author of pioneering school-to-work software for Classroom Inc., a nonprofit organization dedicated to improving reading and math skills for middle and high school learners. She wrote lyrics and music for *SCIENCE SONGS*, which was an American Library Association nominee for notable recording. In addition, she has served on the adjunct faculty of Hunter, Manhattan, and Brooklyn Colleges, teaching courses in science methods, literacy, and writing.

Acknowledgments for Covers

Front cover: *Bones* (bg) ©MedicalRF.com/Photo Researchers, Inc.; *false color X-rays on hand* (l) ©Lester Lefkowitz/Getty Images; *primate* (cl) ©Bruno Morandi/The Image Bank/Getty Images; *red cells* (cr) ©Todd Davidson/Getty Images; *fossils* (r) ©Yoshihi Tanaka/amana images/Getty Images

Michael R. Heithaus

Director, School of Environment and Society
Associate Professor, Department of Biological Sciences
Florida International University
North Miami, Florida

Mike Heithaus joined the Florida International University Biology Department in 2003. He has served as Director of the Marine Sciences Program and is now Director of the School of Environment and Society, which brings together the natural and social sciences and humanities to develop solutions to today's environmental challenges. While earning his doctorate, he began the research that grew into the Shark Bay Ecosystem Project in Western Australia, with which he still works. Back in the United States, he served as a Research Fellow with National Geographic, using remote imaging in his research and hosting a 13-part *Crittercam* television series on the National Geographic Channel. His current research centers on predator-prey interactions among vertebrates, such as tiger sharks, dolphins, dugongs, sea turtles, and cormorants.

Donna M. Ogle

Professor of Reading and Language
National-Louis University
Chicago, Illinois

Creator of the well-known KWL strategy, Donna Ogle has directed many staff development projects translating theory and research into school practice in middle and secondary schools throughout the United States. She is a past president of the International Reading Association and has served as a consultant on literacy projects worldwide. Her extensive international experience includes coordinating the Reading and Writing for Critical Thinking Project in Eastern Europe, developing an integrated curriculum for a USAID Afghan Education Project, and speaking and consulting on projects in several Latin American countries and in Asia. Her books include *Coming Together as Readers; Reading Comprehension: Strategies for Independent Learners; All Children Read;* and *Literacy for a Democratic Society.*

Program Reviewers

Content Reviewers

Paul D. Asimow, PhD
Professor of Geology and Geochemistry
Division of Geological and Planetary Sciences
California Institute of Technology
Pasadena, CA

Laura K. Baumgartner, PhD
Postdoctoral Researcher
Molecular, Cellular, and Developmental Biology
University of Colorado
Boulder, CO

Eileen Cashman, PhD
Professor
Department of Environmental Resources Engineering
Humboldt State University
Arcata, CA

Hilary Clement Olson, PhD
Research Scientist Associate V
Institute for Geophysics, Jackson School of Geosciences
The University of Texas at Austin
Austin, TX

Joe W. Crim, PhD
Professor Emeritus
Department of Cellular Biology
The University of Georgia
Athens, GA

Elizabeth A. De Stasio, PhD
Raymond H. Herzog Professor of Science
Professor of Biology
Department of Biology
Lawrence University
Appleton, WI

Dan Franck, PhD
Botany Education Consultant
Chatham, NY

Julia R. Greer, PhD
Assistant Professor of Materials Science and Mechanics
Division of Engineering and Applied Science
California Institute of Technology
Pasadena, CA

John E. Hoover, PhD
Professor
Department of Biology
Millersville University
Millersville, PA

William H. Ingham, PhD
Professor (Emeritus)
Department of Physics and Astronomy
James Madison University
Harrisonburg, VA

Charles W. Johnson, PhD
Chairman, Division of Natural Sciences, Mathematics, and Physical Education
Associate Professor of Physics
South Georgia College
Douglas, GA

Program Reviewers *(continued)*

Tatiana A. Krivosheev, PhD
Associate Professor of Physics
Department of Natural Sciences
Clayton State University
Morrow, GA

Joseph A. McClure, PhD
Associate Professor Emeritus
Department of Physics
Georgetown University
Washington, DC

Mark Moldwin, PhD
Professor of Space Sciences
Atmospheric, Oceanic, and
Space Sciences
University of Michigan
Ann Arbor, MI

Russell Patrick, PhD
Professor of Physics
Department of Biology,
Chemistry, and Physics
Southern Polytechnic State
University
Marietta, GA

Patricia M. Pauley, PhD
*Meteorologist, Data Assimilation
Group*
Naval Research Laboratory
Monterey, CA

Stephen F. Pavkovic, PhD
Professor Emeritus
Department of Chemistry
Loyola University of Chicago
Chicago, IL

L. Jeanne Perry, PhD
Director (Retired)
Protein Expression Technology
Center
Institute for Genomics and
Proteomics
University of California, Los
Angeles
Los Angeles, CA

Kenneth H. Rubin, PhD
Professor
Department of Geology and
Geophysics
University of Hawaii
Honolulu, HI

Brandon E. Schwab, PhD
Associate Professor
Department of Geology
Humboldt State University
Arcata, CA

Marllin L. Simon, Ph.D.
Associate Professor
Department of Physics
Auburn University
Auburn, AL

Larry Stookey, PE
Upper Iowa University
Wausau, WI

Kim Withers, PhD
Associate Research Scientist
Center for Coastal Studies
Texas A&M University-Corpus
Christi
Corpus Christi, TX

Matthew A. Wood, PhD
Professor
Department of Physics & Space
Sciences
Florida Institute of Technology
Melbourne, FL

Adam D. Woods, PhD
Associate Professor
Department of Geological
Sciences
California State University,
Fullerton
Fullerton, CA

Natalie Zayas, MS, EdD
Lecturer
Division of Science and
Environmental Policy
California State University,
Monterey Bay
Seaside, CA

Teacher Reviewers

Ann Barrette, MST
Whitman Middle School
Wauwatosa, WI

Barbara Brege
Crestwood Middle School
Kentwood, MI

**Katherine Eaton Campbell,
M Ed**
Chicago Public Schools-Area 2
Office
Chicago, IL

**Karen Cavalluzzi, M Ed,
NBCT**
Sunny Vale Middle School
Blue Springs, MO

Katie Demorest, MA Ed Tech
Marshall Middle School
Marshall, MI

Jennifer Eddy, M Ed
Lindale Middle School
Linthicum, MD

Tully Fenner
George Fox Middle School
Pasadena, MD

Dave Grabski, MS Ed
PJ Jacobs Junior High School
Stevens Point, WI

Amelia C. Holm, M Ed
McKinley Middle School
Kenosha, WI

Ben Hondorp
Creekside Middle School
Zeeland, MI

George E. Hunkele, M Ed
Harborside Middle School
Milford, CT

Jude Kesl
Science Teaching Specialist 6–8
Milwaukee Public Schools
Milwaukee, WI

Joe Kubasta, M Ed
Rockwood Valley Middle School
St. Louis, MO

Mary Larsen
Science Instructional Coach
Helena Public Schools
Helena, MT

Angie Larson
Bernard Campbell Middle School
Lee's Summit, MO

Christy Leier
Horizon Middle School
Moorhead, MN

Helen Mihm, NBCT
Crofton Middle School
Crofton, MD

Jeff Moravec, Sr., MS Ed
Teaching Specialist
Milwaukee Public Schools
Milwaukee, WI

**Nancy Kawecki Nega, MST,
NBCT, PAESMT**
Churchville Middle School
Elmhurst, IL

Mark E. Poggensee, MS Ed
Elkhorn Middle School
Elkhorn, WI

Sherry Rich
Bernard Campbell Middle School
Lee's Summit, MO

Mike Szydlowski, M Ed
Science Coordinator
Columbia Public Schools
Columbia, MO

Nichole Trzasko, M Ed
Clarkston Junior High School
Clarkston, MI

Heather Wares, M Ed
Traverse City West Middle School
Traverse City, MI

Contents
in Brief

Your skin is an organ, and like a suit of armor, it protects you from all kinds of things in the environment.

Contents

The 206 bones in our skeletal system not only protect our organs, but they also help us move, store minerals, and make blood cells for us.

© Houghton Mifflin Harcourt Publishing Company • Image Credits: (l) ©Stockbyte/Getty Images; (r) ©Digital Vision/Getty Images

Assignments:

_____

_____

_____

_____

_____

Giardia lamblia is only one of the many parasites found in water that can make us sick.

Giardia lamblia

Power up with *Science Fusion!*

Your program fuses . . .

e-Learning and Virtual Labs

Labs and Activities

Write-In Student Edition

. . . to generate energy for today's science learner — you.

Write-In Student Edition

Be an active reader and make this book your own!

You can answer questions, ask questions, create graphs, make notes, write your own ideas, and highlight information right in your book.

Learn science concepts and skills by interacting with every page.

Labs and Activities

ScienceFusion includes lots of exciting hands-on inquiry labs and activities, each one designed to bring science skills and concepts to life and get you involved.

By asking questions, testing your ideas, organizing and analyzing data, drawing conclusions, and sharing what you learn...

You are the scientist!

e-Learning and Virtual Labs

Digital lessons and virtual labs provide e-learning options for every lesson of Science Fusion.

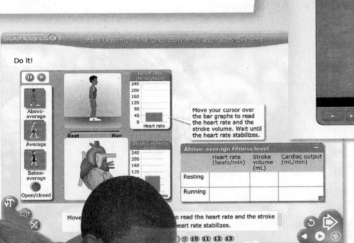

On your own or with a group, explore science concepts in a digital world.

360° of Inquiry

Human Body Systems

Big Idea

The human body is made up of systems that have different functions, and these systems work together to maintain the body.

A brain scan can show whether the brain is functioning normally.

A patient must stay still to get an accurate MRI scan.

What do you think?

In the Middle Ages, people dug up and dissected the dead to learn about the body. Today, technology like the MRI scanner allows us to study the living body. How does the living body work?

Unit 1
Human Body Systems

Muscles at Work

Design a test for muscle endurance or strength.

① Define The Problem

Unlike many things that wear out with use, our muscles actually get stronger the more often they are used. Doing different kinds of exercises helps different groups of muscles. But how can you tell if you are improving? How can you tell how strong a group of muscles are?

Muscles become larger as they become stronger.

Strength moves like this hold take practice and training.

② Think About It

Design a test for a group of muscles.

Choose a group of muscles that you would like to work with. Then, come up with one or two simple exercises that can be done to show either how strong the muscles are or how well they are able to work continuously. Place a time limit on your tests so that the tests don't take too long.

Check off the points below as you use them to design your test.

☐ The kind of action the muscles can do.

☐ To do the test safely, remember to isolate the group of muscles. (Research how to do an exercise safely.)

☐ The equipment you will need for the test.

③ Plan and Test Your Design

A Write out how you will conduct your test in the space below. Check your plan with your teacher before proceeding.

_____
_____
_____
_____
_____

B Conduct the test on yourself. Have a classmate time you, help you count, or make any other measurements that you might need help with. Briefly state your findings.

_____
_____
_____
_____
_____

Take It Home

Do the same exercises at home for two weeks. Do strength training exercises every second day to avoid injury. Do continuous movement exercises, such as running, every day. Then, conduct your test again. See if there is any improvement. Report your findings to the class.

Introduction to Body Systems

ESSENTIAL QUESTION

How do the body systems work together to maintain homeostasis?

By the end of this lesson, you should be able to describe the functions of the human body systems, including how they work together to maintain homeostasis.

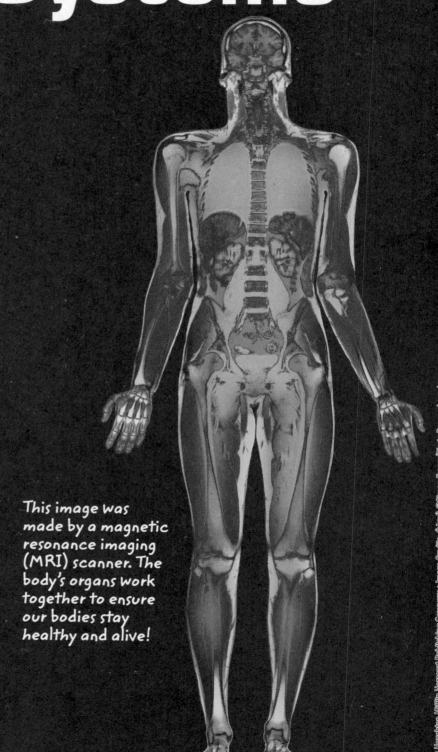

This image was made by a magnetic resonance imaging (MRI) scanner. The body's organs work together to ensure our bodies stay healthy and alive!

Engage Your Brain

1 Predict Check T or F to show whether you think each statement is true or false.

T	F	
☒	☐	Your muscles provide a framework that supports and protects your body.
☒	☐	When you breathe in and out, you're using your lungs.
☐	☒	Your nervous system gets rid of wastes from your body.
☒	☐	When you eat food, it enters your digestive system.

2 Identify Draw a diagram of your body showing at least four organs. As you read the lesson, write down the organ system that each organ is a part of.

✏️ Active Reading

3 Synthesize You can often define an unknown word if you know the meaning of its word parts. Use the word parts and sentence below to make an educated guess about the meaning of the word *homeostasis*.

Greek word	Meaning
homoios	same
stasis	standing

Example Sentence
In order to maintain <u>homeostasis</u>, the cardiovascular system and the respiratory system work together to move oxygen-carrying blood around the body.

homeostasis:

_____

_____

_____

_____

Vocabulary Term

- **homeostasis**

4 Apply As you learn the definition of the vocabulary term in this lesson, make a sketch that shows the meaning of the term or an example of that term. Next to your drawing, write your own definition of the term.

What do the body systems do?

Humans and other organisms need to get energy. They need to use energy to run their bodies and move. They need to reproduce. They need to get rid of waste and protect their bodies. Body systems, also called *organ systems*, help organisms to do all of these things. They also coordinate all the functions of a body.

Groups of organs that work together form body systems. Nerves detect a stimulus in the environment and send a signal through the spinal cord to the brain. The brain sends a signal to respond. Without all the parts, the system would not work. Some organs work in more than one organ system.

Active Reading **5 Identify** As you read about body systems on these pages, underline the main function of each body system.

The respiratory system gathers oxygen from the environment and gets rid of carbon dioxide from the body. The exchange occurs in the lungs.

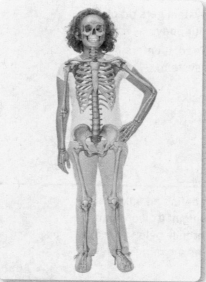

The muscular system allows movement of body parts. It works with the skeletal system to help you move.

The skeletal system is made up of bones, ligaments, and cartilage. It supports the body and protects important organs. It also makes blood cells.

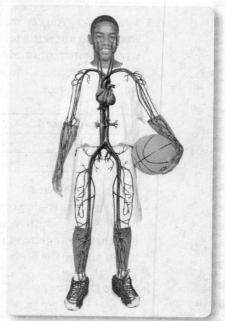

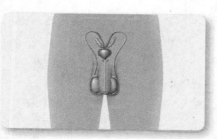

The male reproductive system produces sperm and delivers it to the female reproductive system.

The female reproductive system produces eggs and nourishes a developing fetus.

The cardiovascular system moves blood through the body. The heart is the pump for this system. Blood flows through blood vessels.

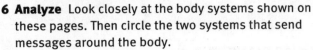
6 Analyze Look closely at the body systems shown on these pages. Then circle the two systems that send messages around the body.

The lymphatic system returns leaked fluid back to the blood. As a major part of the immune system, it has cells that help get rid of invading bacteria and viruses.

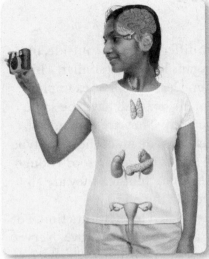

The endocrine system makes chemical messages. These messages help to regulate conditions inside the body. They also influence growth and development.

The integumentary system is the protective covering of the body. It includes the skin, hair, and nails. As part of the immune system, the skin acts as a barrier that protects the body from infection.

The excretory system gets rid of the body's wastes. The urinary system, shown here, removes wastes from blood. The skin, lungs, and digestive system also remove wastes from the body.

The digestive system breaks down food into nutrients that can be used by the body. The stomach breaks down food into tiny pieces. Nutrients are absorbed in the small intestine.

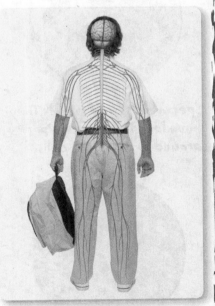

The nervous system collects information and responds to it by sending electrical messages. This information may come from outside or inside the body. The brain is the center of the nervous system.

A Closer Look

How are structure and function linked?

Even though animals may look very different on the outside, on the inside, their cells, tissues, and organs look very similar. This is because these structures do the same basic job. For example, a frog's heart, a bird's heart, and a human's heart all have the same function, to pump blood around the body. They are all made of the same type of muscle tissue, which is made up of the same type of muscle cells. The structure of the hearts is similar, too. Though their shape may be a little different from each other, they are all muscular pumps that push blood around the body.

The shapes and sizes of cells are related to their function. For example, sperm cells have long tails that are used to move. Nerve cells are long and thin to send messages long distances. Surface skin cells are broad and flat. The diagram below shows how skin cells form the skin, which covers and protects the body.

Sperm cells can "swim." They have long tails that whip around to move the cells.

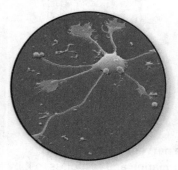

Nerve cells have long, thin branches to send electrical messages between the brain and far-away body parts.

Skin is made up of different cells in many layers. The epidermis is the outer layer of skin. The dermis is the second layer of skin and contains glands, hair follicles, and blood vessels.

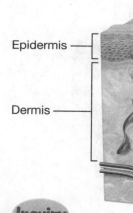

Epidermis

Dermis

Inquiry

7 Infer Muscle cells can get longer and shorter. How does this ability fit in with their job in the body?

_____

_____

_____

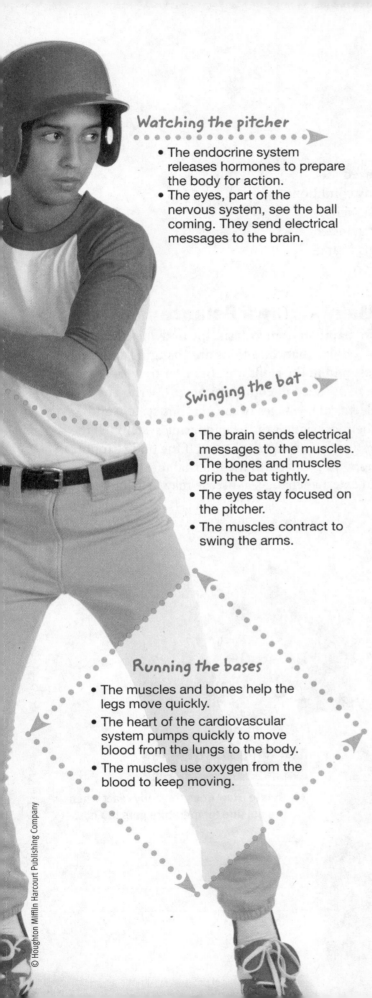

Watching the pitcher ▶
- The endocrine system releases hormones to prepare the body for action.
- The eyes, part of the nervous system, see the ball coming. They send electrical messages to the brain.

Swinging the bat ▶
- The brain sends electrical messages to the muscles.
- The bones and muscles grip the bat tightly.
- The eyes stay focused on the pitcher.
- The muscles contract to swing the arms.

Running the bases
- The muscles and bones help the legs move quickly.
- The heart of the cardiovascular system pumps quickly to move blood from the lungs to the body.
- The muscles use oxygen from the blood to keep moving.

How do body systems work together?

Our body systems can do a lot, but they can't work alone! Almost everything we need for our bodies to work properly requires many body systems to work together. For example, the nervous system may sense danger. The endocrine system releases hormones that cause the heart to beat faster to deliver more oxygen through the circulatory system to muscles. The muscular system and skeletal system work together to run away from danger.

Active Reading **8 Identify** As you read the captions on the left, underline examples of body systems working together.

Body Systems Share Organs

Many organs are part of several body systems. Reproductive organs are part of the reproductive system and part of the endocrine system. The liver works in the digestive system but also is part of the excretory system. The heart is part of the muscular system and the cardiovascular system. Blood vessels too are shared. For example, blood vessels transport chemical messages from the endocrine system and cells from the lymphatic and cardiovascular systems.

Body Systems Communicate

There are two basic ways cells communicate: by electrical messages and by chemical messages. Nerve cells transfer information between the body and the spinal cord and brain. Nerves pass electrical messages from one cell to the next along the line. The endocrine system sends chemical messages through the bloodstream to certain cells.

9 Apply When you are finished running the bases, you are sweating and you feel thirsty. What body systems are interacting in this case?

_____

_____

_____

Keeping the Balance

What is homeostasis?

Cells need certain conditions to work properly. They need food and oxygen and to have their wastes taken away. If body conditions were to change too much, cells would not be able to do their jobs. **Homeostasis** (hoh•mee•oh•STAY•sis) is the maintenance of a constant internal environment when outside conditions change. Responding to change allows all systems to work properly.

Responding to Change

If the external environment changes, body systems work together to keep conditions stable within the body. For example, if body cells were to get too cold, they would not work properly and they could die. So, if the brain senses the body temperature is getting too low, it tells the muscles to shiver. Shivering muscles release energy as heat which warms the body. Your brain will also tell you to put on a sweater!

Maintaining a Balance

To maintain homeostasis, the body has to recognize that conditions are changing and then respond in the right way. In order to work, organ systems need to communicate properly. The electrical messages of the nervous system and chemical signals of the endocrine system tell the body what changes to make. If the body cannot respond properly to the internal messages or to an external change, a disease may develop.

Too cold

Just right

Too hot

A thermostat keeps an even temperature in a room by turning the heater off when it gets too warm, and on when it gets too cold. Your body does the same thing but in a different way.

Visualize It!

10 Relate How does the body react when the outside temperature gets too hot?

_____

_____

_____

_____

What can go wrong with homeostasis?

If one body system does not work properly, other body systems can be affected. For example, body cells that do not get enough energy or nutrients cannot work properly. A lack of food harms many systems and may cause disease or even death. The presence of toxins or pathogens also can disrupt homeostasis. Toxins can prevent cells from carrying out life processes and pathogens can break down cells. Problems also occur if the body's messages do not work, or they are not sent when or where they are needed. Many diseases which affect homeostasis are hereditary.

11 Identify As you read this page, underline what can happen if homeostasis is disrupted.

Structure or Function Diseases

Problems with the structure or function of cells, tissues, or organs can affect the body. For example, diabetes is a disease that affects cell function. Certain changes in body cells stop them from taking glucose in from the blood as they normally do. If cells cannot get energy in the form of glucose, they cannot work properly.

Pathogens and Disease

When the body cannot maintain homeostasis, it is easier for pathogens to invade the body. Pathogens can also cause a disruption in homeostasis. For example, tuberculosis is a lung disease caused by bacteria. It weakens the lungs and body. Weakened lungs cannot take in oxygen well. Low oxygen levels affect the whole body.

12 Apply Alcoholism is a disease that disrupts homeostasis. Below are three body systems that are affected by alcohol. The effects on the nervous system are filled in. In the space provided, predict what might happen when the function of the two remaining systems is affected.

Body systems affected	What are the effects?
Nervous system	Disrupts proper functioning of the brain. The brain cannot respond properly to internal or external messages.
Digestive system	
Reproductive system	

Alcoholism can damage the structure and function of the liver and reduce its ability to remove toxins from the blood.

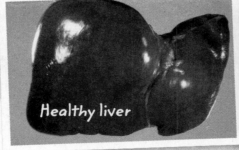

Healthy liver

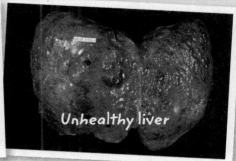

Unhealthy liver

Visual Summary

To complete this summary, fill in the blanks with the correct word or phrase. Then use the key below to check your answers. You can use this page to review the main concepts of the lesson.

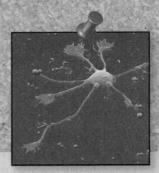

Body systems each have specific jobs.

13 The _____ system brings oxygen into the blood and releases carbon dioxide from the body.

The structure of cells, tissues, and organs are linked to their functions.

14 The long, thin cells of the _____ system help transmit electrical messages around the body.

The muscular heart pushes _____ around the body.

Body Systems and Homeostasis

Body systems work together, which allows the body to work properly.

15 The _____ and _____ systems work together to allow the player to swing the bat.

The body maintains homeostasis by adjusting to change.

16 If body temperature goes up, the _____ senses the change and will work to reduce the body temperature to normal.

Answers: 13 respiratory; 14 nervous; blood; 15 nervous; muscular (either order) 16 brain

17 Explain How might disruption of the respiratory system affect homeostasis of the body?

Lesson Review

Vocabulary

Use a term from the lesson to complete each sentence below.

1 _____ is maintaining stable conditions inside the body.

2 A group of organs that work together is called a(n) _____ .

Key Concepts

3 Compare How are the functions of the skeletal and muscular systems related?

_____
_____
_____

4 Identify What body system receives information from inside and outside the body and responds to that information?

_____
_____

5 Explain How is skin part of the integumentary system and the excretory system?

_____
_____
_____
_____

6 Describe What are the basic needs of all cells in the body?

_____
_____
_____

7 Relate Give an example of how a cell's structure relates to its function in the body.

_____
_____
_____
_____

Critical Thinking

Use the graph to answer the following questions.

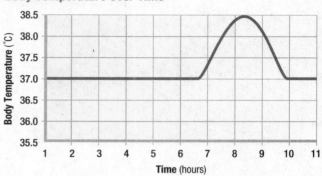

Body Temperature over Time

8 Analyze Is the body in homeostasis during the entire time shown in the graph? Explain your answer.

_____
_____
_____

9 Predict What would happen to the body if the body temperature continued to decrease during the tenth hour instead of leveling off?

_____
_____
_____

10 Apply The body loses water and salts in sweat. Explain why drinking large volumes of plain water after exercising may affect the salt balance in the body.

_____
_____
_____
_____
_____

My Notes

The Skeletal and Muscular Systems

ESSENTIAL QUESTION

How do your skeletal and muscular systems work?

By the end of this lesson, you should be able to explain how the skeletal and muscular systems work together to allow movement of the body.

By working together, your muscular and skeletal systems allow you to do many things such as stand up, sit down, type a note, or run a race.

Lesson Labs

Quick Labs
• Power in Pairs
• Speed of a Reflex

Exploration Lab
• A Closer Look at Muscles

Engage Your Brain

1 Identify Circle the terms that best complete the following sentences.

The *skeletal / muscular* system is responsible for supporting the body.

Bones are part of your *skeletal / muscular* system.

Your heart is made up of *bone / muscle* tissue.

You can increase your flexibility by stretching your *bones / muscles*.

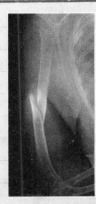

2 Infer This x-ray shows a broken arm. How might this injury affect your ability to move?

_____

_____

_____

_____

 ## Active Reading

3 Synthesize You can often identify functions of a body part if you know what its name means. Use the Latin words below and context clues to make an educated guess about a function of *ligaments* and *tendons*.

Latin word	Meaning
ligare	to tie
tendere	to stretch

Example Sentence
Ligaments are found at the ends of bones.

ligament:

_____

Example Sentence
Tendons connect muscles to bones.

tendon:

_____

Vocabulary Terms
• skeletal system
• ligament
• joint
• muscular system
• tendon

4 Apply As you learn the definition of each vocabulary term in this lesson, create your own definition or sketch it to help you remember the meaning of the term.

What's Inside?

What are the main functions of the skeletal system?

When you hear the word *skeleton*, you might think of the dry, white bones that you see in the models in your science class. You might think your bones are lifeless, but they are very much alive. The **skeletal system** is the organ system that supports and protects the body and allows it to move. Its other jobs include storing minerals and producing red blood cells. A human's skeleton is inside the body, so it is called an *endoskeleton*.

Active Reading

5 Identify As you read, underline the main functions of the skeletal system.

Visualize It!

6 Relate How might a suit of armor be a good analogy for a function of the skeletal system?

A suit of armor, like the skeletal system protects the body.

Protection

Bones provide protection to organs. For example, your ribs protect your heart and lungs, your vertebrae protect your spinal cord, and your skull protects your brain.

Storage

The hard outer layer of bone, called *compact bone*, stores important minerals such as calcium. These minerals are necessary for nerves and muscles to work properly.

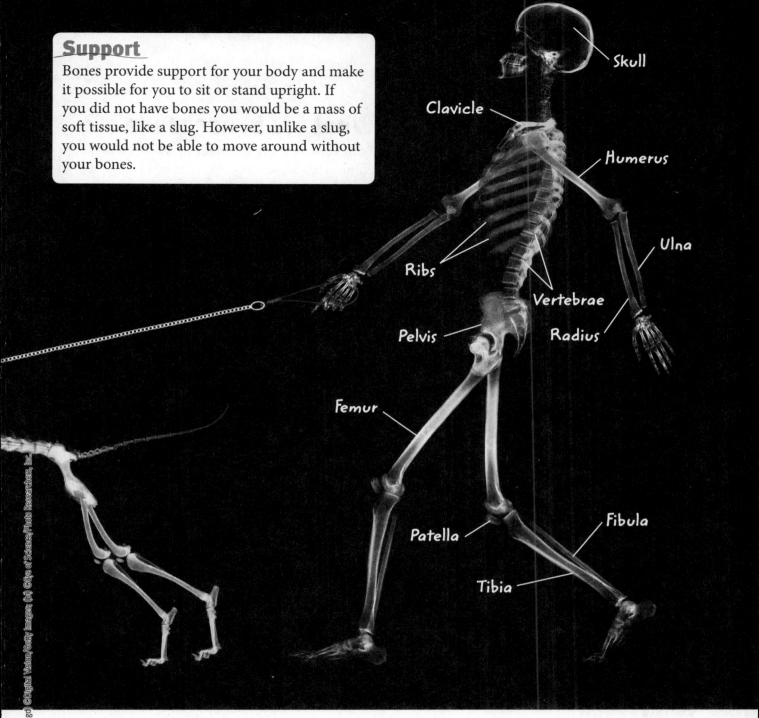

Support

Bones provide support for your body and make it possible for you to sit or stand upright. If you did not have bones you would be a mass of soft tissue, like a slug. However, unlike a slug, you would not be able to move around without your bones.

Skull

Clavicle

Humerus

Ulna

Ribs

Vertebrae

Radius

Pelvis

Femur

Fibula

Patella

Tibia

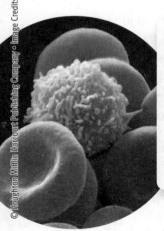

Blood Cell Production

At the center of bones, such as the long bones in the man's and dog's legs, is soft tissue called *marrow*. Red marrow, a type of marrow that makes blood cells, is found mostly in flat bones such as the ribs, pelvis and skull. The red and white blood cells shown here are made in the red bone marrow.

Movement

Bones play an important role in movement by providing a place for muscles to attach. Muscles pull on bones to move the body. Without bones, muscles could not do their job of moving the body.

No Bones About It!

What are the parts of the skeletal system?

Bones, ligaments, and cartilage make up your skeletal system. The skeletal system is divided into two parts. The skull, vertebrae, and ribs make up the *axial skeleton*, which supports the body's weight and protects internal organs. The arms, legs, shoulders, and pelvis make up the *appendicular skeleton*, which allows for most of the body's movement.

Bones

Bones are alive! They have blood vessels which supply nutrients and nerves which signal pain. The body of a newborn baby has about 300 bones, but the average adult has only 206 bones. As a child grows, some bones fuse together.

Ligaments

The tough, flexible strand of connective tissue that holds bones together is a **ligament**. Ligaments allow movement, and are found at the end of bones. Some ligaments, such as the ones on your vertebrae, prevent too much movement of bones.

7 Compare How does the axial skeleton differ from the appendicular skeleton?

The axil skeleton supports the body's weight and protects organs, but, the appendicular skeleton provides movement.

Cartilage

Cartilage is a strong, flexible, and smooth connective tissue found at the end of bones. It allows bones to move smoothly across each other. The tip of your nose and your ears are soft and bendy because they contain only cartilage. Cartilage does not contain blood vessels.

What are bones made of?

Bones are hard organs made of minerals and connective tissue. If you looked inside a bone, you would notice two kinds of bone tissue. One kind, called *compact bone*, is dense and does not have any visible open spaces. Compact bone makes bones rigid and hard. Tiny canals within compact bone contain blood capillaries. The other kind of bone tissue, called *spongy bone*, has many open spaces. Spongy bone provides most of the strength and support for a bone. In long bones, such as those of the arm or the leg, an outer layer of compact bone surrounds spongy bone and another soft tissue called *marrow*.

Active Reading **8 Identify** As you read, underline the name of a protein found in bone.

Minerals

Calcium is the most plentiful mineral in bones. The minerals in bones are deposited by bone cells called *osteoblasts*. Minerals such as calcium make the bones strong and hard.

Connective Tissue

The connective tissue in bone is made mostly of a protein called <u>collagen</u>. Minerals make the bones strong and hard, but the collagen in bones allows them to be flexible enough to withstand knocks and bumps. Otherwise, each time you bumped a bone, it would crack like a china cup.

Marrow

Bones also contain a soft tissue called *marrow*. There are two types of marrow. Red marrow is the site of platelet and red and white blood cell production. Red marrow is in the center of flat bones such as the ribs. Yellow marrow, which is found in the center of long bones such as the femur, stores fat.

Bones, such as the femur shown here, are made mostly of connective tissue. They also contain minerals such as calcium.

Ligament
Spongy bone
Compact bone
Marrow
Blood vessels
Cartilage

9 Summarize In the chart below, fill in the main functions of each part of the skeletal system.

Structure	Function
Spongy bone	Provides strength and support
Compact bone	Makes the bone rigid and hard
Cartilage	Allows bones to move smoothly across each other
Ligaments	Holds bones together.

How do bones grow?

The skeleton of a fetus growing inside its mother's body does not contain hard bones. Instead, most bones start out as flexible cartilage. When a baby is born, it still has a lot of cartilage. As the baby grows, most of the cartilage is replaced by bone.

The bones of a child continue to grow. The long bones lengthen at their ends, in areas called *growth plates*. Growth plates are areas of cartilage that continue to make new cells. Bone cells called *osteocytes* move into the cartilage, hardening it and changing it into bone. Growth continues into adolescence and sometimes even into early adulthood. Most bones harden completely after they stop growing. Even after bones have stopped growing, they can still repair themselves if they break.

This baby's skeleton has more cartilage than his older brother's skeleton has.

Bone Connections

How are bones connected?

The place where two or more bones connect is called a **joint**. Some joints allow movement of body parts, others stop or limit movement. Just imagine how difficult it would be to do everyday things such as tying your shoelaces if you could not bend the joints in your arms, legs, neck, or fingers!

Joints

Bones are connected to each other at joints by strong, flexible ligaments. The ends of the bone are covered with cartilage. Cartilage is a smooth, flexible connective tissue that helps cushion the area in a joint where bones meet. Some joints allow little or no movement. These *fixed joints* can be found in the skull. Other joints, called *movable joints*, allow movement of the bones.

Your joints allow you to do everyday tasks easily.

Some Examples of Movable Joints

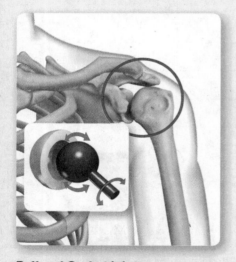

Ball and Socket joint
Shoulders and hips are ball-and-socket joints. Ball-and-socket joints allow one of the bones of the joint to rotate in a large circle.

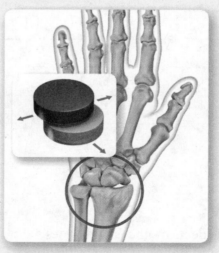

Gliding joint
Wrists and ankles are gliding joints. Gliding joints allow a great deal of flexibility in many directions.

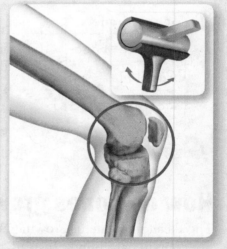

Hinge joint
Knees and elbows are hinge joints. Hinge joints work like door hinges, allowing bones to move back and forth.

10 **Apply** Some joints, such as the ones in your skull, do not move at all. Why do you think it is important that skull joints cannot move?

If your skull moved, your brain would be exposed.

What are some injuries and disorders of the skeletal system?

Sometimes the skeletal system can become injured or diseased. Injuries and diseases of the skeletal system affect the body's support system and ability to move. Hereditary factors may play a role in the incidence of diseases such as osteoporosis and arthritis.

 **Active Reading**

11 Identify As you read, underline the characteristics of each injury and disease.

Fractures

Bones may be fractured, or broken. Bones can be broken by a high-force impact such as a fall from a bike. A broken bone usually repairs itself in six to eight weeks.

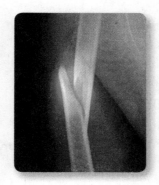

Sprains

A sprain is an injury to a ligament that is caused by stretching a joint too far. The tissues in the sprained ligament can tear and the joint becomes swollen and painful to move. Sprains are common sports injuries.

12 Apply How could someone sprain a ligament?

Someone could sprain a
ligment by twisting your
ankle.

Osteoporosis

Osteoporosis is a disease that causes bone tissue to become thin. The bones become weak and break more easily. It is most common among adults who do not get enough calcium in their diet. What you eat now can affect your risk of developing osteoporosis later in life.

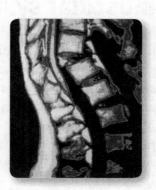

13 Infer Why is it important to get enough calcium in your diet?

Without calcium, your bones
will become thin and weak

Arthritis

Arthritis is a disease that causes joints to swell, stiffen, and become painful. It may also cause the joint to become misshapen, as shown in the photo. A person with arthritis finds it difficult to move the affected joint. Arthritis can be treated with drugs that reduce swelling.

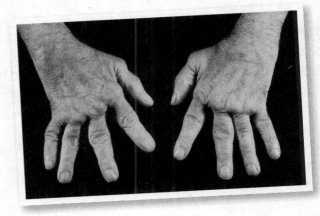

Keep Moving!

What are the main functions of the muscular system?

Muscles pump blood through your body, enable you to breathe, hold you upright, and allow you to move. All animals except the simplest invertebrates have muscles for movement. The **muscular system** is mostly made of the muscles that allow your body to move and be flexible. Other muscles move materials inside your body. *Muscle* is the tissue that contracts and relaxes, making movement possible. Muscle tissue is made up of muscle cells. Muscle cells contain special proteins that allow them to shorten and lengthen.

Active Reading 14 **Identify** How do muscles make movement possible?

_____

_____

_____

What are the three types of muscles?

Your body has three kinds of muscle tissue: *skeletal muscle, smooth muscle*, and *cardiac muscle*. Each muscle type has a specific function in your body.

You are able to control the movement of skeletal muscle, so it is called *voluntary muscle*. You are not able to control the movement of smooth muscle and cardiac muscles. Muscle action that is not under your control is *involuntary*. Smooth muscle and cardiac muscle are called *involuntary muscles*.

Smooth Muscle

Smooth muscle is found in internal organs and blood vessels. It helps move materials through the body. Arteries and veins contain a layer of smooth muscle that can contract and relax. This action controls blood flow through the blood vessel. Smooth muscle movement in your digestive system helps move food through your intestines. Smooth muscle is involuntary muscle.

Smooth muscle cells are spindle shaped. They are fat in the middle with thin ends.

Cardiac muscle cells are long, thin, and branched.

Cardiac Muscle

Cardiac muscle is the tissue that makes up the heart. Your heart never gets tired like your skeletal muscle can. This is because cardiac muscle cells are able to contract and relax without ever getting tired. In order to supply lots of energy to the cells, cardiac muscle cells contain many mitochondria. Your cardiac muscles do not stop moving your entire lifetime!

The contractions of cardiac muscle push blood out of the heart and pump it around the body. Cardiac muscle is involuntary; you cannot consciously stop your heart from pumping.

Skeletal Muscle

Skeletal muscle cells are long and thin with stripes, or striations.

Skeletal muscle is attached to your bones and allows you to move. You have control over your skeletal muscle. For example, you can bring your arm up to your mouth to take a bite from an apple. The tough strand of tissue that connects a muscle to a bone is called a **tendon**. When a muscle contracts, or shortens, the attached bones are pulled closer to each other. For example, when the bicep muscle shortens, the arm bends at the elbow.

Most skeletal muscles work in pairs around a joint, as shown below. One muscle in the pair, called a *flexor*, bends a joint. The other muscle, the *extensor*, straightens the joint. When one muscle of a pair contracts, the other muscle relaxes to allow movement of the body part. Muscle pairs are found all around the body.

Visualize It!

15 Apply What would happen to the arm if the flexor was not able to contract?

_____

_____

_____

_____

_____

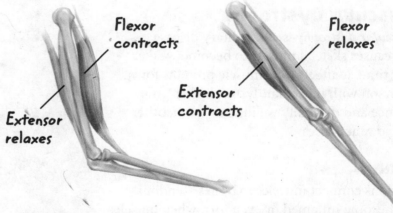

Flexor contracts

Extensor relaxes

Flexor relaxes

Extensor contracts

The biceps muscle is the flexor that contracts to bend the arm.

The triceps muscle is the extensor that contracts to straighten the arm.

Visualize It!

16 Compare How do the three muscle tissue types look similar and different?

_____

_____

_____

_____

Move It or Lose It!

What are some injuries and disorders of the muscular system?

Like other systems, the muscular system can suffer injury or disease. As a result, muscles may lose normal function. Some muscle diseases are hereditary. Diseases that affect muscle function can also affect other body systems. For example, myocarditis is an inflammation of the heart muscle that can cause heart failure and harm the cardiovascular system.

Muscle Strain and Tears

A *strain* is a muscle injury in which a muscle is overstretched or torn. This can happen when muscles have not been stretched properly or when they are overworked. Strains cause the muscle tissue to swell and can be painful. Strains and tears need rest to heal.

Muscular Dystrophy

Muscular dystrophy is a hereditary disease that causes skeletal muscle to become weaker over time. It affects how muscle proteins form. A person with muscular dystrophy has poor balance and difficulty walking or doing other everyday activities.

Tendinitis

Tendons connect muscles to bones. Tendons can become inflamed or even torn when muscles are overused. This painful condition is called *tendinitis*. Tendinitis needs rest to heal. It may also be treated with medicines that reduce swelling.

17 **Contrast** What is the difference between a muscle strain and tendinitis?

_____

_____

_____

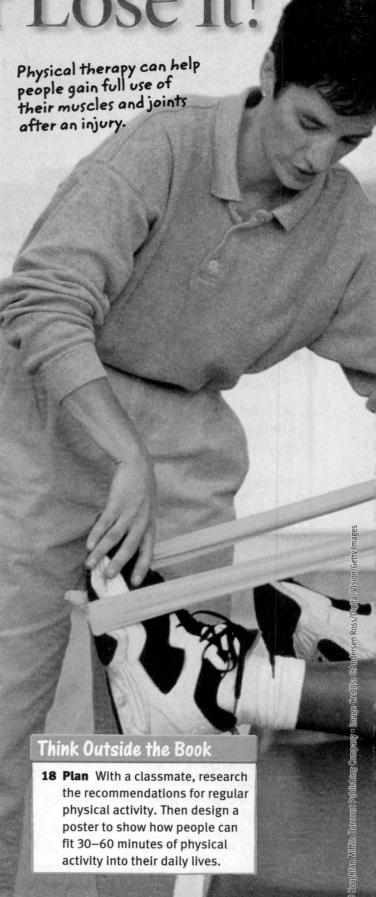

Physical therapy can help people gain full use of their muscles and joints after an injury.

Think Outside the Book

18 **Plan** With a classmate, research the recommendations for regular physical activity. Then design a poster to show how people can fit 30–60 minutes of physical activity into their daily lives.

What are some benefits of exercise?

Exercising is one of the best things you can do to keep your body healthy. *Exercise* is any activity that helps improve physical fitness and health. Exercise benefits the muscular system by increasing strength, endurance, and flexibility. Exercise helps other body systems, too. It helps keep your heart, blood vessels, lungs, and bones healthy. Exercise also reduces stress, helps you sleep well, and makes you feel good.

Exercises that raise your heart rate to a certain level for at least 60 minutes improve the fitness of the heart. A fit heart is a more efficient pump. It can pump more blood around the body with each beat. It is also less likely to develop heart disease. Good muscle strength and joint flexibility may help a person avoid injuries. Weight training helps bones stay dense and strong. Dense, strong bones are less likely to break. Thirty to sixty minutes of physical activity every day can help improve the health of people of all ages, from children to older adults.

 **Active Reading** **19 Identify** As you read, underline the characteristics of anaerobic and aerobic exercise.

Muscle Strength

Resistance exercise helps improve muscle strength by building skeletal muscle and increasing muscle power. Resistance exercise involves short bursts of intense effort lasting no more than a few minutes. Resistance exercises are also called *anaerobic exercises* because the muscle cells contract without using oxygen. Lifting weights and doing pushups are examples of anaerobic exercises.

Muscle Endurance

Endurance exercises allow muscles to contract for a longer time without getting tired. Endurance exercises are also called *aerobic exercises* because the muscle cells use oxygen when contracting. Aerobic exercises involve moderately intense activity from about 30 to 60 minutes at a time. Some examples of aerobic exercises are walking, jogging, bicycling, skating, and swimming.

Flexibility

Can you reach down and touch your toes? If a joint can move through a wide range of motions, it has good flexibility. *Flexibility* refers to the full range of motion of a joint. Stretching exercises help improve flexibility of a joint. Having good flexibility can help prevent ligament, tendon, and muscle injuries. Stretching after aerobic or anaerobic exercises may also help prevent injuries.

Visual Summary

To complete this summary, fill in the blanks with the correct word or phrase. Then, use the key below to check your answers. You can use this page to review the main concepts of the lesson.

The Skeletal and Muscular Systems

The skeletal system supports and protects the body and allows for movement.

20 The three main parts of the skeletal system are bones, _cartalige_, and _ligments_.

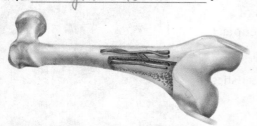

Joints connect two or more bones.

21 The shoulder is an example of a _ball and socket_ joint.

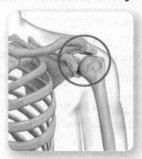

The muscular system allows for movement and flexibility.

22 Muscles work in _pairs_ to move body parts.

Exercise benefits the body in many ways.

23 Aerobic exercises improve muscle _endurance_.
Anaerobic exercises improve muscle _strength_.

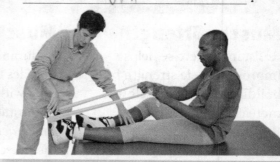

Answers: 20 cartilage; ligaments; 21 ball and socket; 22 pairs; 23 endurance; strength

24 **Synthesize** Explain why you need both muscles and bones to move your body.

Lesson Review

Vocabulary

Draw a line to connect the following terms to their definitions.

1 skeletal system

2 ligament

3 muscular system

4 joint

5 tendon

A groups of muscles that allow you to move and that move materials inside your body

B a place where two or more bones connect

C bones, cartilage, and the ligaments that hold bones together

D tough strands of tissue that connect muscles to bones

E a type of tough, flexible connective tissue that holds bones together

Key Concepts

6 List What are the functions of the skeletal system?

Protect organs
Provide movement
Provide Structure

7 Analyze What are bones made of?

Blood, Calcium, marrow

8 Explain How do muscles work in pairs to move the body?

When the extensor contracts
(straight arm) the
flexor relaxes
When the flexor contracts, (bent
arm), the exensor relaxes

9 Identify What bone disease is caused by a lack of calcium in the diet?

Osteoporoses

Critical Thinking

Use this graph to answer the following questions.

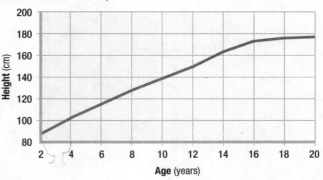

Growth Chart of a Boy

10 Analyze At which points in this graph is bone growing at the fastest rate?

2   20

11 Infer At which times on this graph would you expect that the boy's growth plates have stopped creating new bone?

20

12 Apply If aerobic exercise improves heart strength so that it pumps more blood with each beat, what likely happens to the heart rate as the cardiac muscle gets stronger? Explain your answer.

My Notes

The Circulatory and Respiratory Systems

ESSENTIAL QUESTION

How do the circulatory and respiratory systems work?

By the end of this lesson, you should be able to relate the structures of the circulatory and respiratory systems to their functions in the human body.

This micrograph shows red blood cells inside a blood vessel in the lung. The blood cells are picking up oxygen to bring to the rest of the body.

Engage Your Brain

1 Identify Check T or F to show whether you think each statement is true or false.

T	F	
☐	☐	Air is carried through blood vessels.
☐	☐	The cardiovascular system does not interact with any other body system.
☐	☐	The respiratory system gets rid of carbon dioxide from the body.
☐	☐	Smoking cigarettes can lead to lung disease.

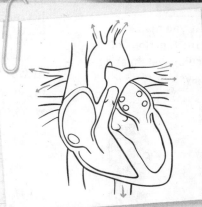

2 Identify What is the name of the organ, shown here, that makes the "lub-dub" sound in your chest?

_____

3 Infer What is the function of this organ?

_____

_____

_____

Active Reading

4 Synthesize You can sometimes tell a lot about the structure of an unknown object by understanding the meaning of its name. Use the meaning of the Latin word and the sentence below to write your own definition of *capillary*.

Latin word	Meaning
capillaris	thin and hairlike

Example Sentence
Oxygen that is carried by blood cells moves across the <u>capillary</u> wall and into body cells.

capillary:

_____

_____

_____

_____

Vocabulary Terms

- **cardiovascular system**
- **blood**
- **lymphatic system**
- **lymph**
- **lymph node**
- **artery**
- **capillary**
- **vein**
- **respiratory system**
- **pharynx**
- **larynx**
- **trachea**
- **bronchi**
- **alveoli**

5 Apply As you learn the definition of each vocabulary term in this lesson, create your own definition or sketch to help you remember the meaning of the term.

Go with the Flow!

What is the circulatory system?

Active Reading

6 Identify As you read, underline the functions of the cardiovascular system and the lymphatic system.

When you hear the term *circulatory system*, what do you think of? If you said "heart, blood, and blood vessels," you are half right. The term circulatory system describes both the cardiovascular system and the lymphatic system. Both systems work closely together to move fluids around your body and protect it from disease. Your moving blood helps to keep all parts of your body warm. In these ways the two systems help maintain homeostasis.

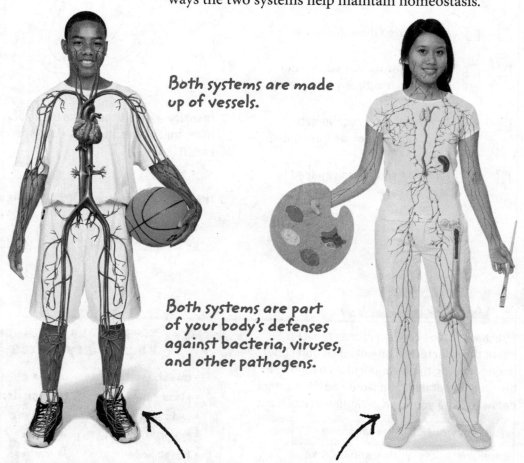

Both systems are made up of vessels.

Both systems are part of your body's defenses against bacteria, viruses, and other pathogens.

The Cardiovascular System

Your heart, blood, and blood vessels make up your **cardiovascular system**, which transports blood around your body. **Blood** is the fluid that carries gases, nutrients, and wastes through the body. The cardiovascular system is a closed circulatory system; the blood is carried in vessels that form a closed loop. The blood maintains homeostasis by transporting hormones, nutrients, and oxygen to cells and by carrying wastes away from cells.

The Lymphatic System

The **lymphatic system** is a group of organs and tissues that collect the fluid that leaks from blood and returns it to the blood. The leaked fluid is called **lymph**. The lymphatic system is an open circulatory system, and lymph can move in and out of the vessels. The lymphatic system is also part of the body's defenses against disease. Certain lymph vessels in the abdomen move fats from the intestine and into the blood.

7 Compare Fill in the Venn diagram to compare the structures and functions of both these systems. You can add more details as you read more about these systems in this lesson.

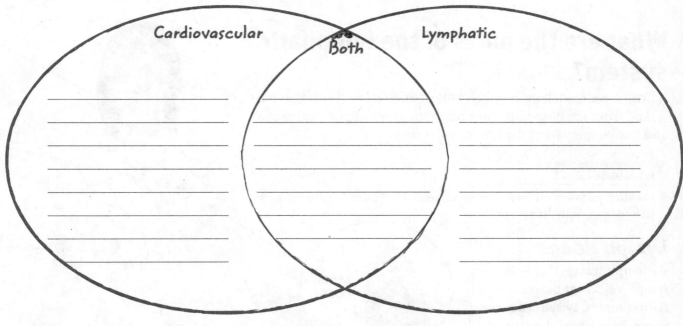

Cardiovascular   Both   Lymphatic

How do the systems work together?

Every time your heart pumps, a little fluid is forced out of the thin walls of the tiniest blood vessels, called *capillaries*. Most of this fluid is reabsorbed by the capillaries, and the remaining fluid is collected by lymph capillaries. *Lymph capillaries* absorb fluid, particles such as dead cells, and pathogens from around body cells. The lymph capillaries carry the fluid, now called *lymph,* to larger lymph vessels. Lymph is returned to the cardiovascular system when it drains into blood vessels at the base of the neck.

The lymphatic system is the place where certain blood cells, called *white blood cells,* mature. Some of these white blood cells stay in the lymphatic system where they attack invading pathogens.

 **Active Reading**

8 Synthesize How does returning leaked fluid from the blood help maintain homeostasis?

_____

_____

_____

_____

_____

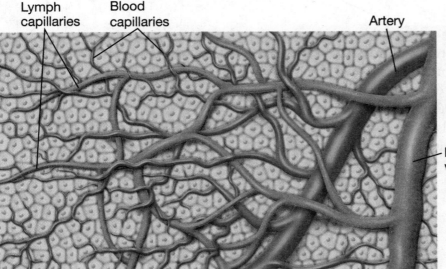

Lymph capillaries   Blood capillaries   Artery

Lymphatic vessel

The fluid that leaks from blood capillaries moves into lymph capillaries and is eventually returned to the blood.

Node Doubt!

What are the parts of the lymphatic system?

As you have read, lymph vessels collect and return fluids that have leaked from the blood. In addition to these vessels, several organs and tissues are part of the lymphatic system.

Active Reading

9 Identify As you read these pages, underline the main function of each part of the lymphatic system.

Lymph Nodes

As lymph travels through lymph vessels, it passes through lymph nodes. **Lymph nodes** are small, bean-shaped organs that remove pathogens and dead cells from lymph. Lymph nodes are concentrated in the armpits, neck, and groin. Infection-fighting blood cells, called *white blood cells,* are found in lymph nodes. When bacteria or other pathogens cause an infection, the number of these blood cells may multiply greatly. The lymph nodes fill with white blood cells that are fighting the infection. As a result, some lymph nodes may become swollen and painful. Swollen lymph nodes might be an early clue of an infection.

Lymph node

Lymph Vessels

Lymph vessels are the thin-walled vessels of the lymphatic system. They carry lymph back to lymph nodes. From the lymph nodes, the fluid is returned to the cardiovascular system through the lymph vessels. The vessels have valves inside them to stop lymph from flowing backward.

Bone Marrow

Bones—part of your skeletal system—are very important to your lymphatic system. *Bone marrow* is the soft tissue inside of bones where blood cells are produced.

Tonsils

Tonsils are small lymphatic organs at the back of the throat and tongue. The tonsils at the back of the throat are the most visible. Tonsils help defend the body against infection. White blood cells in the tonsil tissues trap pathogens. Tonsils in the throat sometimes get infected. An infection of the tonsils is called *tonsillitis*. When tonsils get infected, they may become swollen, as shown here.

Thymus

The *thymus* is an organ in the chest. Some white blood cells made in the bone marrow finish developing in the thymus. From the thymus, the white blood cells travel through the lymphatic system to other areas of the body. The thymus gets smaller as a person gets older. This organ is also a part of the endocrine system.

Spleen

The *spleen* is the largest lymphatic organ. It stores white blood cells and also allows them to mature. As blood flows through the spleen, white blood cells attack or mark pathogens in the blood. If pathogens cause an infection, the spleen may also release white blood cells into the bloodstream.

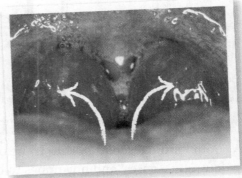

Swollen tonsils

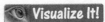 Visualize It!

10 Predict A bad case of tonsillitis can sometimes affect a person's breathing. How is this possible?

_____

_____

_____

What are some disorders of the lymphatic system?

Lymphoma is a type of cancer that often begins in a lymph node. It can cause a swelling in the node called a *tumor*. There are many different types of lymphomas. Another disorder of the lymph system is lymphedema (lim•fih•DEE•muh). Lymphedema is a swelling of body tissues caused by a blockage or injury to lymph vessels. Lymph vessels are unable to drain lymph from a certain area, and that area becomes swollen. Filariasis is a disease caused by threadlike worms called *nematodes*. The nematodes may enter lymphatic vessels and block them, preventing lymph from moving around the body. Bubonic plague is a bacterial infection of the lymphatic system. The bacteria can enter the body through the bite of an infected flea. The bacteria grow inside lymph nodes, causing the nodes to swell.

Active Reading

11 Identify As you read, underline the names of the lymphatic system diseases discussed here.

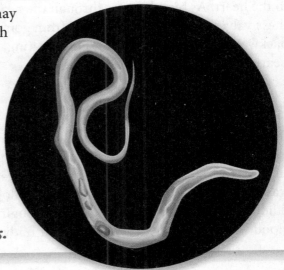

A person gets infected with filarial worms by being bitten by an infected fly. Filariasis is rare in the United States, but is common in developing countries.

The Heart of the Matter

What are the parts of the cardiovascular system?

Your cardiovascular system is the organ system that carries nutrients, gases, and hormones to body cells and waste products from body cells. It also helps keep the different parts of your body at an even temperature. Your cardiovascular system is made up of the heart, blood vessels, and blood.

Heart

The heart is the pump that sends blood around the body. Your heart is about the size of your fist and is almost in the center of your chest. When heart muscle contracts, it squeezes the blood inside the heart. This squeezing creates a pressure that pushes blood through the body.

Your heart has a left side and a right side. The two sides are separated by a thick wall. The right side of the heart pumps oxygen-poor blood to the lungs. The left side pumps oxygen-rich blood to the body. Each side has an upper chamber and a lower chamber. Each upper chamber is called an *atrium*. Each lower chamber is called a *ventricle*. Blood enters the atria and is pumped down to the ventricles. Flaplike structures called *valves* are located between the atria and the ventricles and in places where large vessels are attached to the heart. As blood moves through the heart, these valves close to prevent blood from going backward. The "lub-dub" sound of a beating heart is caused by the valves closing.

Blood

Blood is a type of connective tissue that is part of the cardiovascular system. It serves as a transport system, providing supplies for cells, carrying chemical messages, and removing wastes so cells can maintain homeostasis. Blood contains cells, fluid, and other substances. It travels through miles and miles of blood vessels to reach every cell in your body.

Left Atrium The left atrium receives oxygen-rich blood from the lungs.

Right Atrium The right atrium receives oxygen-poor blood from the body.

Right Ventricle The right ventricle pumps oxygen-poor blood to the lungs.

Left Ventricle The left ventricle pumps oxygen-rich blood to the body.

13 Infer Why is it important for your heart to keep oxygen-rich blood separate from oxygen-poor blood?

_____

_____

_____

_____

_____

Blood Vessels

Blood travels throughout your body in tubes called *blood vessels*. The three types of blood vessels are arteries, capillaries, and veins.

An **artery** is a blood vessel that carries blood away from the heart. Arteries have thick walls with a layer of smooth muscle. Each heartbeat pumps blood into your arteries at high pressure, which is your *blood pressure*. This pressure pushes blood through the arteries. Artery walls are strong and stretch to withstand the pressure. Nutrients, oxygen, and other substances must leave the blood to get to your body's cells. Carbon dioxide and other wastes leave body cells and are carried away by blood. A **capillary** is a tiny blood vessel that allows these exchanges between body cells and the blood. The gas exchange can take place because capillary walls are only one cell thick. Capillaries are so narrow that blood cells must pass through them in single file! No cell in the body is more than three or four cells away from a capillary.

Capillaries lead to veins. A **vein** is a blood vessel that carries blood back to the heart. Blood in veins is not under as much pressure as blood in arteries is. Valves in the veins keep the blood from flowing backward. The contraction of skeletal muscles around veins can help blood move in the veins.

Arteries carry oxygen-rich blood away from the heart.

Capillaries deliver oxygen-rich blood to body cells and take oxygen-poor blood away from body cells.

Veins carry oxygen-poor blood back to the heart.

14 Apply Complete the table below by naming the blood vessels and by sketching their function. Your sketch may be a symbol, as shown here.

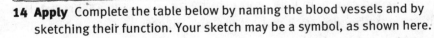

Type of blood vessel		Vein
Sketch of function	♡→	↕

It's in the Blood

What is blood made of?

An adult human body has about 5 liters of blood. Your body probably has a little less than that. Blood is made up of plasma, platelets, and red and white blood cells. Blood is a tissue because it is made of at least two different cell types. If you looked at blood under a microscope, you would see these differently shaped cells and platelets.

The Blood Files

Plasma

The fluid part of the blood is called *plasma*. Plasma is a mixture of water, minerals, nutrients, sugars, proteins, and other substances. This fluid also carries waste. Red blood cells, white blood cells, and platelets are found in plasma.

Platelets

Platelets are tiny pieces of larger cells found in bone marrow. Platelets last for only five to ten days, but they have an important role. When you cut or scrape your skin, you bleed because blood vessels have been cut open. As soon as bleeding starts, platelets begin to clump together in the cut area. They form a plug that helps reduce blood loss. Platelets also release chemicals that react with proteins in plasma. The reaction causes tiny fibers to form. The fibers help create a blood clot.

White Blood Cells

White blood cells help keep you healthy by fighting pathogens such as bacteria and viruses. Some white blood cells squeeze out of blood vessels to search for pathogens. When they find one they destroy it. Other white blood cells form antibodies. *Antibodies* are chemicals that identify pathogens. White blood cells also keep you healthy by destroying body cells that have died or been damaged.

White blood cell

Red blood cell

Platelet

Red Blood Cells

Most blood cells are red blood cells. *Red blood cells* are disk-shaped cells that do not have a nucleus. They bring oxygen to every cell in your body. Cells need oxygen to carry out life functions. Each red blood cell has hemoglobin. *Hemoglobin* is an oxygen-carrying protein; it clings to the oxygen molecules you inhale. Red blood cells can then transport oxygen to cells in every part of the body. The disk shape of red blood cells helps them squeeze into capillaries.

15 Predict How would the body be affected if red blood cells had low levels of hemoglobin?

_____

_____

_____

_____

_____

How does blood move through the body?

Blood is pumped from the right side of the heart to the lungs. From the lungs it returns to the left side of the heart. The blood is then pumped from the left side of the heart to the body. It flows to the tiny capillaries around the body before returning to the right side of the heart. Blood in the arteries that come out of the heart is under great pressure because of the force from the pumping action of the heart. Blood in veins is under much less pressure than arterial blood because veins have larger internal diameters than arteries do. Veins carry larger volumes of blood more slowly.

Blood Moves in Circuits

Blood moves in two loops or circuits around the body. The beating heart moves blood to the lungs and also around the body. The flow of blood between the heart and the lungs is called the *pulmonary circulation*. As blood passes through the lungs, carbon dioxide leaves the blood and oxygen is picked up. The oxygen-rich blood then flows back to the heart, where it is pumped around the rest of the body. The circulation of blood between the heart and the rest of the body is called *systemic circulation*. Oxygen-poor blood returns to the heart from body cells in the systemic circulation.

Active Reading **16 Compare** What is the difference between the pulmonary and systemic circulations?

_____

_____

_____

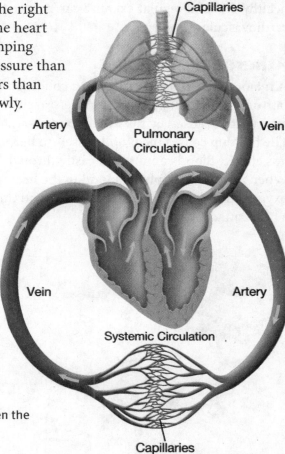

In pulmonary circulation, blood is pumped to the lungs where carbon dioxide leaves the blood and oxygen enters the blood.

Capillaries

Artery

Pulmonary Circulation

Vein

Vein

Artery

Systemic Circulation

Capillaries

In systemic circulation, blood moves around the body.

Visualize It!

17 Apply Put a box around the part of the diagram that shows the pulmonary circulation. Where in the diagram would you find oxygen-poor blood?

_____

_____

_____

_____

How does circulation help maintain body temperature?

The circulation of blood also helps homeostasis. When the brain senses that body temperature is rising, it signals blood vessels in the skin to widen. As the vessels get wider, heat from the blood is transferred to the air around the skin. This transfer helps lower body temperature. When the brain senses that body temperature is normal, it signals the blood vessels to return to normal. When the brain senses the body temperature is getting too low, it signals the blood vessels near the skin to get narrower. This allows the blood to stay close to internal organs to keep them warm.

What are some problems that affect the cardiovascular system?

Cardiovascular disease is the leading cause of death in the United States. Cardiovascular disease can be caused by smoking, poor diet, stress, physical inactivity, or in some cases, heredity. Eating a healthy diet and regular exercise can reduce the risk of developing cardiovascular problems.

Atherosclerosis

A major cause of heart disease is a condition called *atherosclerosis* (ath•uh•roh•skluh•ROH•sis). Atherosclerosis is a hardening of artery walls caused by the build up of cholesterol and other lipids. The buildup causes the blood vessels to become narrower and less elastic. Blood cannot flow easily through a narrowed artery. When an artery supplying blood to the heart becomes blocked, oxygen cannot reach the heart muscle and the person may have a heart attack.

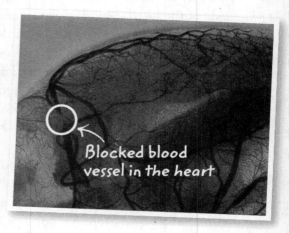
Blocked blood vessel in the heart

Blood pressure checks can help detect illness.

Hypertension

Hypertension is abnormally high blood pressure. Atherosclerosis may be caused in part by hypertension. The higher a person's blood pressure is, the greater their risk of developing cardiovascular problems such as heart attacks and strokes. Hypertension that is not treated can also cause kidney damage and shorten life expectancy. Regular check ups can help detect problems with blood pressure. Hypertension can be controlled with diet and sometimes with medication.

Heart Attacks and Strokes

A heart attack happens when an artery that supplies blood to the heart becomes blocked and the heart muscle tissue that depends on that blood supply does not get oxygen. Cells and tissues that do not get oxygen get damaged and can die. If enough heart muscle cells are damaged, the heart may stop beating.

A stroke can happen when a blood vessel in the brain becomes blocked or bursts. As a result, that part of the brain receives no oxygen. Without oxygen, brain cells die. Brain damage that occurs during a stroke can affect many parts of the body. People who have had a stroke may experience paralysis or difficulty in speaking.

Think Outside the Book Inquiry

18 Research Doctors often use an electrocardiogram (EKG) reading to see if there is something wrong with how a person's heart is beating. An EKG is a type of graph that "draws" the pumping activity of the heart. How might graphing the heartbeat help a doctor tell if there is a problem?

Take a Deep Breath

What are the functions of the respiratory system?

Your cells need a constant supply of oxygen to stay alive. Your cells must also be able to get rid of the waste product carbon dioxide, which is toxic to them. Breathing takes care of both of these needs. The **respiratory system** is the group of organs that takes in oxygen and gets rid of carbon dioxide. *Respiration,* or breathing, is the transport of oxygen from outside the body to cells and tissues, and the transport of carbon dioxide and wastes away from cells and to the environment.

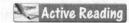
Active Reading

19 Identify As you read this page, underline the gas that is needed by your body for cellular respiration.

Takes in Oxygen

When a person inhales, air is drawn into the lungs. Oxygen in the air moves into the blood from the lungs. The oxygen-rich blood flowing away from the lungs is carried to all the cells in the body. Oxygen leaves the capillaries and enters the body cells. Inside each cell, oxygen is used for cellular respiration. During cellular respiration, the energy that is stored in food molecules is released. Without oxygen, body cells would not be able to survive.

Releases Carbon Dioxide

When a person exhales, carbon dioxide is released from the body. Carbon dioxide is a waste product of cellular respiration, and the body needs to get rid of it. Carbon dioxide moves from body cells and into capillaries where it is carried in the blood all the way to the lungs. Blood that flows to the lungs contains more carbon dioxide than oxygen. The carbon dioxide moves out of the lung capillaries and into the lungs where it is exhaled.

☐ Oxygen
☐ Carbon Dioxide

☐ Oxygen
☐ Carbon Dioxide

Visualize It!

20 Apply Scuba divers breathe air from the tanks strapped to their bodies. Check the box next to the gas you would expect to find in the greatest concentration in the air tank on the diver's back and in the air bubbles he is exhaling.

Breathe Easy

What are the parts of the respiratory system?

Breathing is made possible by your respiratory system. Air enters your respiratory system through your nose or mouth when you breathe in. From there, the air moves through a series of tubes to get to your lungs.

Nose, Pharynx, and Larynx

Air enters your respiratory system through your nose and your mouth. From the nose, air flows into the **pharynx** (FAIR•ingks), or throat. The pharynx branches into two tubes. One tube, the *esophagus*, leads to the stomach. The other tube, called the *larynx,* leads to the lungs. The **larynx** (LAIR•ingks) is the part of the throat that holds the vocal cords. When air passes across the vocal cords, they vibrate, making the voice.

Trachea

The larynx is connected to a large tube called the **trachea** (TRAY•kee•uh), or windpipe. Air flows from the larynx through the trachea to the lungs. The trachea splits into two branches called **bronchi** (singular, *bronchus*). One bronchus connects to each lung. Each bronchus branches into smaller tubes called *bronchioles*.

Bronchioles and Alveoli

In the lungs, the bronchioles lead to tiny sacs called **alveoli** (singular, *alveolus*). Alveoli are surrounded by blood vessels. Gases in the air move across the thin walls of the alveoli and blood vessels. As you breathe, air is sucked into and forced out of alveoli. Breathing is carried out by the diaphragm and rib muscles. The *diaphragm* is a dome-shaped muscle below the lungs. As you inhale, the diaphragm contracts and moves down. The volume of the chest increases. As a result, a vacuum is created and air is sucked in. Exhaling reverses this process.

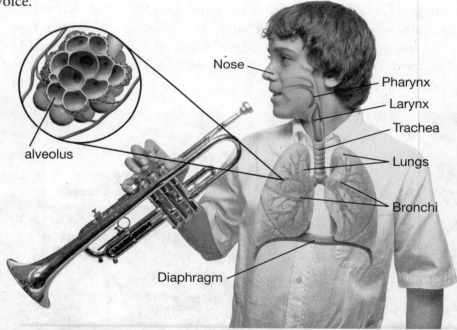

alveolus

Nose
Pharynx
Larynx
Trachea
Lungs
Bronchi
Diaphragm

Visualize It!

21 Apply Draw arrows showing the direction of air flow into the lungs. How would an object blocking a bronchus affect this airflow?

_____

_____

What are some disorders of the respiratory system?

Millions of people suffer from respiratory disorders. These disorders include asthma, pneumonia, emphysema, and lung cancer. Some respiratory problems such as emphysema and lung cancer are strongly linked to cigarette smoke. Other respiratory disorders such as pneumonia are caused by pathogens, and some are genetic disorders. Depending on the cause, there are many different ways to treat respiratory diseases.

Active Reading

22 Identify As you read, underline the characteristics of the different respiratory disorders.

Asthma

Asthma is a condition in which the airways are narrowed due to inflammation of the bronchi. During an asthma attack, the muscles in the bronchi tighten and the airways become inflamed. This reduces the amount of air that can get into or out of the lungs. Asthma is treated with medicines that open the bronchioles.

Pneumonia

Pneumonia (noo•MOHN•yuh) is an inflammation of the lungs that is usually caused by bacteria or viruses. Inflamed alveoli may fill with fluid. If the alveoli are filled with too much fluid, the person cannot take in enough oxygen and he or she may suffocate. Pneumonia can be treated with medicines that kill the pathogens.

Emphysema

Emphysema (em•fuh•SEE•muh) occurs when the alveoli have been damaged. As a result, oxygen cannot pass across into the blood as well as it could in a normal alveolus. People who have emphysema have trouble getting the oxygen they need and removing carbon dioxide from the lungs. This condition is often linked to long-term use of tobacco.

Visualize It!

23 Compare How are these two lungs different? How can you tell the diseased lung from the healthy lung?

_____

_____

_____

_____

Think Outside the Book

24 Imagine Pretend you are a lung. The behavior of your body has not been very healthy, and as a result you are sick. Write a plea to your body to help you improve your health. Be sure to include the important functions that you perform and what the body can do to make you healthier.

Emphysema lung

Healthy lung

Visual Summary

To complete this summary, fill in the blanks with the correct word or phrase. Then use the key below to check your answers. You can use this page to review the main concepts of the lesson.

The lymphatic system returns fluid to the blood.

25 The lymph organs found in your throat are called

_____.

Circulatory and Respiratory Systems

The cardiovascular system moves blood throughout the body and carries nutrients and oxygen to body cells.

26 The two gases that the blood carries around the body are

_____ and

_____.

The respiratory system takes oxygen into the body and releases carbon dioxide.

27 Oxygen enters the blood and carbon dioxide leaves the blood in the

_____ of the lungs.

Answers: 25 tonsils; 26 oxygen, carbon dioxide; 27 alveoli

28 Relate Describe how a problem with the respiratory system could directly affect the cardiovascular system.

Lesson Review

Vocabulary

In your own words, define the following terms.

1 Blood

_____

_____

2 Lymph

_____

_____

3 Alveoli

_____

_____

Key Concepts

Fill in the table below.

System	Structures
4 Identify What are the main structures of the lymphatic system?	
5 Identify What are the main structures of the cardiovascular system?	
6 Identify What are the main structures of the respiratory system?	

7 Explain How does blood help maintain homeostasis in the body?

_____

_____

_____

8 Contrast How are arteries and veins different?

_____

_____

_____

_____

9 Relate How might a blockage of the lymph vessels affect the function of the cardiovascular system?

_____

_____

_____

_____

Critical Thinking

Use this image to answer the following questions.

Arterial wall   Fatty deposit

10 Relate To what body system does this structure belong?

_____

11 Predict How might what is happening in this image affect the nervous system?

_____

_____

_____

12 Infer Why is it important that lymph vessels are spread throughout the body?

_____

_____

_____

My Notes

Olufunmilayo Falusi Olopade

MEDICAL DOCTOR

Dr. Olufunmilayo Olapade is the head of the University of Chicago's Cancer Risk Clinic. The MacArthur Foundation awarded her $500,000 for her creative work in breast cancer research.

Born in Nigeria, Dr. Olopade began her career as a medical officer at the Nigerian Navy Hospital in Lagos. She later came to Chicago to do cancer research. She became a professor at the University of Chicago in 1991. She founded the Cancer Risk Clinic shortly after this.

Dr. Olopade has found that tumors in African-American women often come from a different group of cells than they do in Caucasian women.

These tumors, therefore, need different treatment. Dr. Olopade designs treatments that address the source of the tumor. More importantly, her treatments try to address the particular risk factors of each patient. These can include diet, heredity, age, and activity. The MacArthur Foundation recognized Dr. Olopade for designing such new and practical treatment plans for patients. Studying cells has provided Dr. Olopade with clues on how to improve the lives of millions of African-American women.

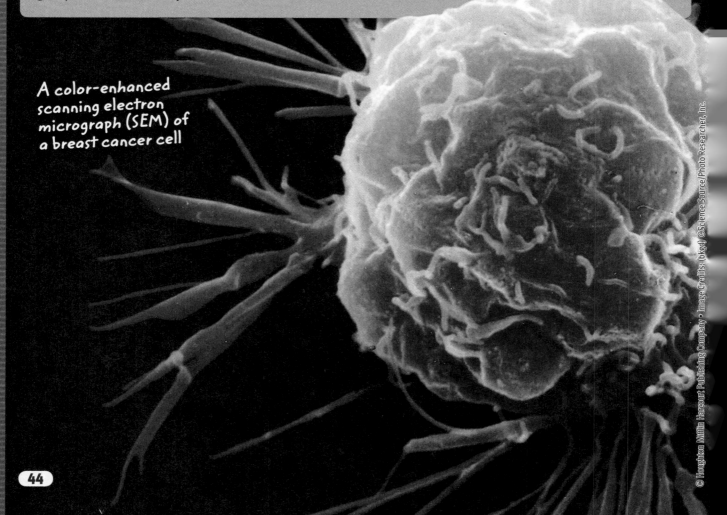

A color-enhanced scanning electron micrograph (SEM) of a breast cancer cell

JOB BOARD

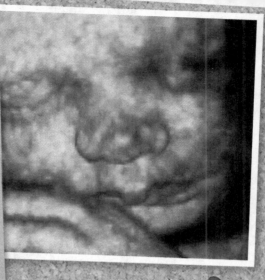

Diagnostic Medical Sonographer

What You'll Do: Operate and take care of the sonogram equipment that uses sound waves to create pictures of inside human bodies that a doctor can interpret.

Where You Might Work: Hospitals, clinics, and private offices that have sonogram equipment.

Education: A two- or four-year undergraduate degree or a special certification program is necessary.

Physical Therapist

What You'll Do: Use exercise, ultrasound, heat, and other treatments when working with patients to help them improve their muscular strength, endurance, and flexibility.

Where You Might Work: Hospitals, clinics, and private physiotherapy offices, as well as some gyms and yoga studios.

Education: A master's degree from an accredited physical therapy program is required.

Prosthetics Technician

What You'll Do: Create, test, fit, maintain, and repair artificial limbs and other prosthetic devices for people who need them.

Where You Might Work: Hospitals with prosthetic divisions and private companies.

Education: Technicians must have an associate, bachelor's, or post-graduate degree in orthotics and prosthetics. Some companies may require additional certification.

Language Arts Connection

Find one report of a new discovery in cancer prevention. Summarize the key points of the discovery in a paragraph. Be sure to include information about what the discovery is, who made it, how the discovery was made, and how it changes what we know about cancer.

The Digestive and Excretory Systems

ESSENTIAL QUESTION

How do your body's digestive and excretory systems work?

By the end of this lesson, you should be able to relate the parts of the digestive and excretory systems to their roles in the human body.

Your digestive system works to get all of the nutrients out of the food you eat.

Lesson Labs

Quick Labs
- Bile Function
- Peristalsis Race
- Mechanical Digestion

S.T.E.M. Lab
- Modeling a Kidney

 Engage Your Brain

1 Predict Fill in the blanks with the words that you think best complete the following sentences.

Inside your _____, food is chewed and broken down by teeth and saliva.

The _____ is a muscle inside your mouth that helps you to swallow food and liquids.

If you eat too much food too quickly, you may get a _____ache.

2 Imagine How is a blender like your stomach?

_____

_____

_____

_____

 Active Reading

3 Synthesize You can often define an unknown word if you see it used in a sentence. Use the sentence below to make an educated guess about the meaning of the word *enzyme*.

Example sentence
Enzymes in the mouth, stomach, and small intestine help in the chemical digestion of food.

enzyme:

_____

_____

_____

_____

Vocabulary Terms

- **digestive system**
- **enzyme**
- **esophagus**
- **stomach**
- **small intestine**
- **large intestine**
- **pancreas**
- **liver**
- **excretory system**
- **kidney**
- **nephron**
- **urine**

4 Apply As you learn the meaning of each vocabulary term in this lesson, create your own definition or sketch to help you remember the meaning of the term.

You are what you eat!

Active Reading

5 Identify As you read, underline the ways that your body uses nutrients.

What is the digestive system?

Your cells need a lot of energy for their daily activities. Cells use nutrients, which are substances in food, for energy, growth, maintenance, and repair. The **digestive system** breaks down the food you eat into nutrients that can be used as building materials and that can provide energy for cells.

The digestive system interacts with other body systems to obtain and use energy from food. Blood, part of the circulatory system, transports nutrients to other tissues. In order to extract energy from nutrients, cells need oxygen. The respiratory system is responsible for obtaining this oxygen from the environment. The nervous system controls and regulates the functioning of the digestive system.

What are the two types of digestion?

Digestion is the process of breaking down food into a form that can pass from the digestive system into the bloodstream. There are two types of digestion: mechanical and chemical.

The Stomach

The deep pits and grooves in the stomach lining help grind food.

Inquiry

6 Infer The stomach lining is made up of deep muscular grooves. How do you think these structures help the stomach to break down food?

_____

_____

_____

_____

Mechanical Digestion

Mechanical digestion is the breaking, crushing, and mashing of food. Chewing is a type of mechanical digestion. Chewing creates small pieces of food that are easier to swallow and digest than large pieces are. Mechanical digestion increases the surface area of food for the action of chemical digestion.

Chemical Digestion

Chemical digestion is the process in which large molecules of food are broken down into smaller molecules so that they can pass into the bloodstream. An **enzyme** (EN•zym) is a chemical that the body uses to break down large molecules into smaller molecules. Enzymes act like chemical scissors. They "cut up" large molecules into smaller pieces. Mechanical digestion breaks up food and increases surface area so that enzymes can break nutrients into smaller molecules. Without mechanical digestion, chemical digestion would take days instead of hours!

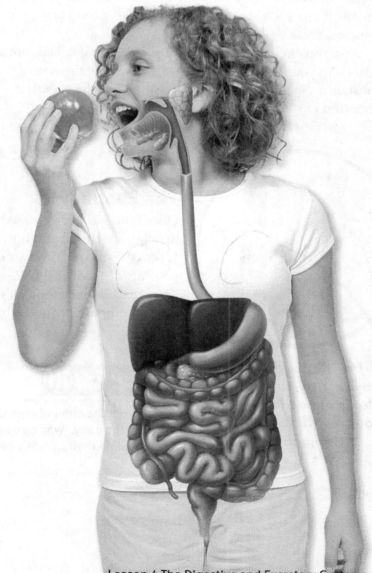

Visualize It!

7 Categorize Decide whether each of these steps in digestion is an example of mechanical digestion or chemical digestion. Then put a check in the correct box.

In your mouth, teeth grind food.

☐ mechanical

☐ chemical

Salivary glands release a liquid called saliva, which helps to break food down.

☐ mechanical

☐ chemical

In the stomach, muscles contract to grind food into a pulpy mixture.

☐ mechanical

☐ chemical

In the small intestine, most nutrients are broken down by enzymes.

☐ mechanical

☐ chemical

Chew on this

What are the parts of the digestive system?

Has anyone ever reminded you to chew your food? Chewing food is the first part of digestion. After food is chewed and swallowed, pieces of that food move through other organs in the digestive system, where the food is broken down even more.

 **Active Reading**

8 As you read, underline the function of each organ of the digestive system.

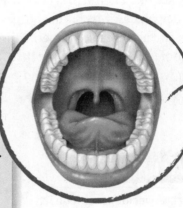

The Mouth

Digestion begins in the mouth with both mechanical and chemical digestion. Teeth, with the help of strong jaw muscles, break and crush food.

As you chew, food is moistened by a liquid called *saliva*. Glands in your mouth make saliva. Saliva contains many substances, including an enzyme that begins the chemical digestion of starches in food.

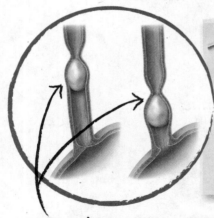

Muscles in the esophagus move this clump of food from your mouth to your stomach.

The Esophagus

Once food has been chewed, it is swallowed. The food moves through the throat and into a long tube called the **esophagus** (ih•SAWF•uh•gus). Waves of muscle contractions called *peristalsis* (per•ih•STAWL•sis) move the food into the stomach. The muscles move food along in much the same way as you move toothpaste from the bottom of the tube with your thumbs.

Visualize It!

9 Infer Consider the order of organs in the digestive system and their positions in the body. Why do you think digestion is more efficient if you are sitting up, rather than slumped over or lying down?

_____

_____

_____

_____

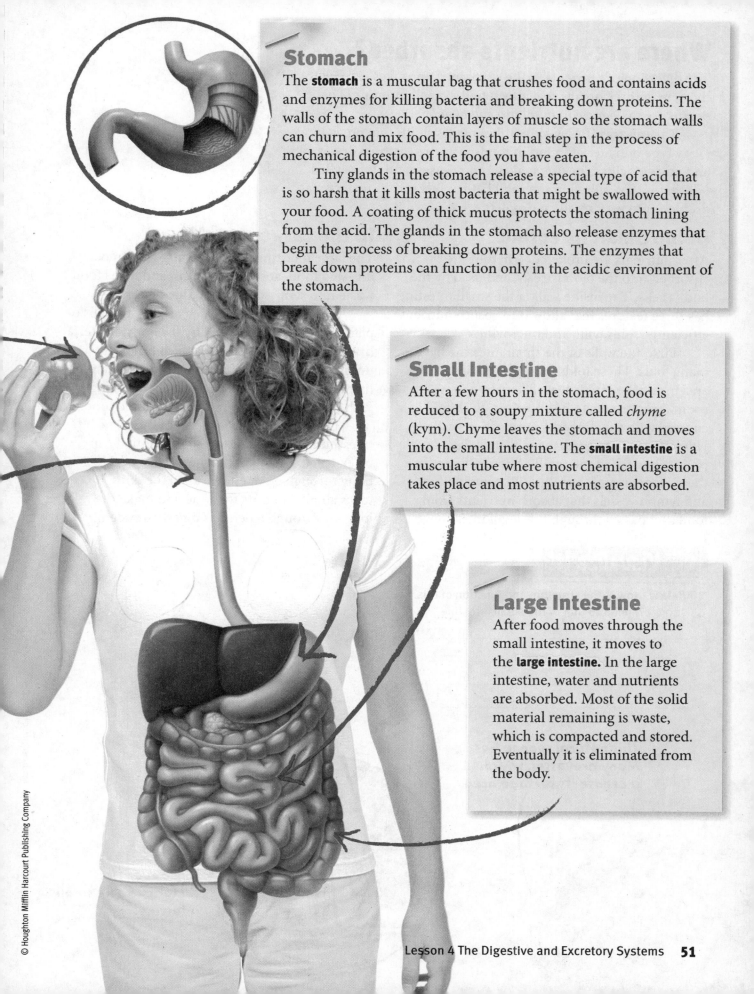

Stomach

The **stomach** is a muscular bag that crushes food and contains acids and enzymes for killing bacteria and breaking down proteins. The walls of the stomach contain layers of muscle so the stomach walls can churn and mix food. This is the final step in the process of mechanical digestion of the food you have eaten.

Tiny glands in the stomach release a special type of acid that is so harsh that it kills most bacteria that might be swallowed with your food. A coating of thick mucus protects the stomach lining from the acid. The glands in the stomach also release enzymes that begin the process of breaking down proteins. The enzymes that break down proteins can function only in the acidic environment of the stomach.

Small Intestine

After a few hours in the stomach, food is reduced to a soupy mixture called *chyme* (kym). Chyme leaves the stomach and moves into the small intestine. The **small intestine** is a muscular tube where most chemical digestion takes place and most nutrients are absorbed.

Large Intestine

After food moves through the small intestine, it moves to the **large intestine.** In the large intestine, water and nutrients are absorbed. Most of the solid material remaining is waste, which is compacted and stored. Eventually it is eliminated from the body.

Where are nutrients absorbed?

The digestion of nutrients in the small intestine takes place with the help of three organs that attach to the small intestine. These organs are the *pancreas*, *liver*, and *gall bladder*.

The **pancreas** (PANG•kree•uhz) makes fluids that break down every type of material found in foods: proteins, carbohydrates, fats, and nucleic acids. The **liver** makes and releases a mixture called *bile* that is then stored in the gall bladder. Bile breaks up large fat droplets into very small fat droplets.

In the Small Intestine

After nutrients are broken down, they are absorbed into the bloodstream and used by the body's cells. The inside wall of the small intestine has three features that allow it to absorb nutrients efficiently: folds, villi, and microvilli.

First, the walls of the small intestine have many folds. These folds increase the surface area inside the intestine wall, creating more room for nutrients to be absorbed. Each fold is covered with tiny fingerlike projections called *villi* (VIL•eye). In turn, the villi are covered with projections called microvilli. Microvilli increase the surface area of the villi. Villi contain blood and lymph vessels that absorb nutrients from food as it passes through the small intestine.

In the Large Intestine

The large intestine removes water from mostly-digested food, absorbs vitamins, and turns food waste into semi-solid waste called feces.

Some parts of food, such as the cell walls of plants, cannot be absorbed by the body. Bacteria live in the large intestine that feed off of this undigested food. The bacteria produce vitamins that are absorbed by the large intestine along with most of the water in the undigested food.

The *rectum* is the last part of the large intestine. The rectum stores feces until it can be expelled. Feces pass to the outside of the body through an opening called the *anus*. It takes about 24 hours for a meal to make the full journey through a person's digestive system.

Visualize It!

10 Relate How is the structure and function of this sponge similar to that of the small intestine?

_____

_____

_____

_____

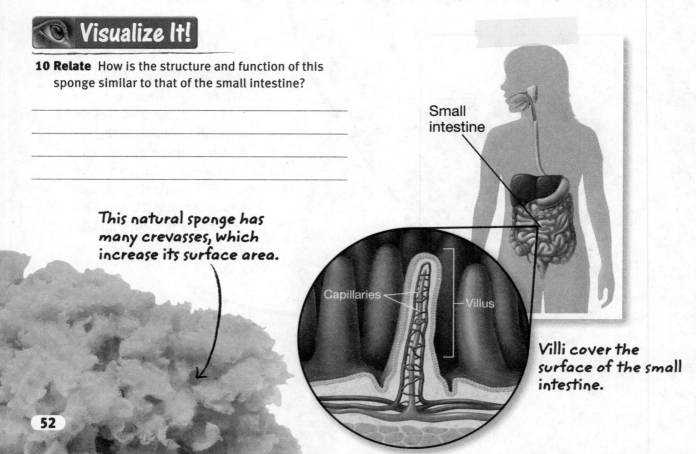

This natural sponge has many crevasses, which increase its surface area.

Small intestine

Capillaries — Villus

Villi cover the surface of the small intestine.

Toxic Waste!

What are the functions of the excretory system?

You have toxic waste in your body! As your cells perform the chemical activities that keep you alive, waste products, such as carbon dioxide and ammonia, are made. These waste products are toxic to cells. If waste builds up in a cell, homeostasis will be disrupted and the cell may die. The **excretory system** eliminates cellular wastes from the body through the lungs, skin, kidneys, and digestive system.

Waste Removal

After you read the text, answer the associated questions below.

To Sweat

Your skin is part of the excretory and the integumentary systems. Waste products such as excess salts are released through your skin when you sweat.

11 Identify Sweat releases wastes through your _____

To Exhale

Your lungs are part of the excretory and respiratory systems. Lungs release water and toxic carbon dioxide when you exhale.

12 List Two waste products that are released when you exhale are _____ and _____

To Produce Urine and Feces

Kidneys, part of the urinary system, remove all types of cellular waste products from your blood. Your digestive system eliminates feces from your body.

13 Identify The urinary system filters waste out of your

_____

Cleanup crew

What organs are in the urinary system?

The urinary system collects cellular waste and eliminates it from the body in the form of liquid waste. Waste products enter the urinary system through the kidneys.

Active Reading

14 Identify As you read, underline the functions of the organs in the urinary system.

Kidneys

The **kidney** is one of a pair of organs that remove waste from the blood. Inside each kidney are more than 1 million microscopic structures called **nephrons** (NEF•rahnz). Fluid is filtered from the blood into the nephron through a structure called the glomerulus (gloh•MEHR•yuh•luhs). Filtered blood leaves the glomerulus and circulates around the tubes that make up the nephron. These structures return valuable salts and ions to the blood. Tubes in the kidneys collect the wastes from the nephrons. Water and the wastes filtered out of the blood form a liquid known as **urine.**

Ureters

Urine forms in the kidneys. From the kidneys, urine travels through the *ureters.* The ureters are tubes that connect the kidneys to the bladder.

Bladder

The urine is transported from the kidneys to the bladder. The bladder is a saclike organ that stores urine. Voluntary muscles hold the urine until it is ready to be released. At that time, the muscles contract and squeeze urine out of the bladder.

Urethra

Urine exits the bladder through a tube called the urethra.

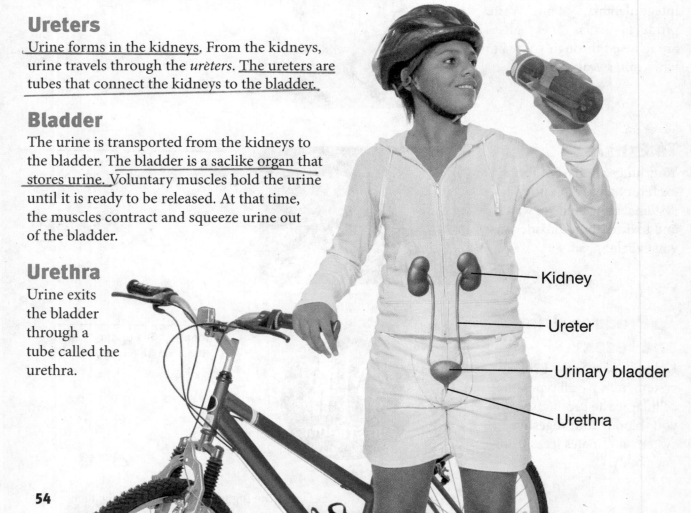

Kidney

Ureter

Urinary bladder

Urethra

Filtering Blood

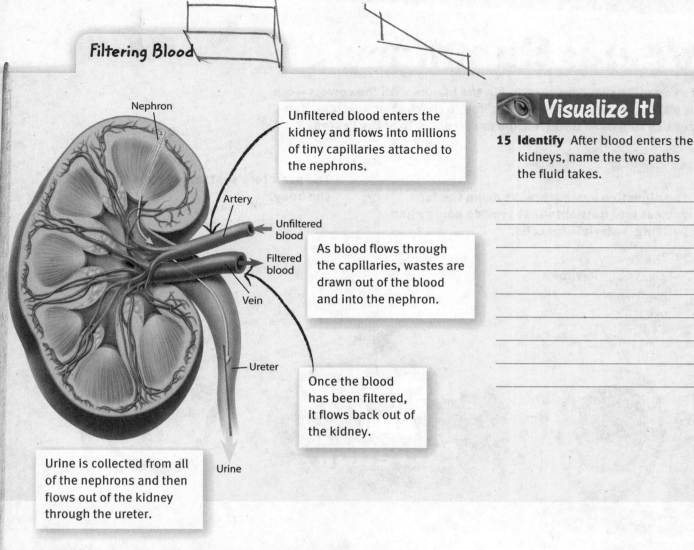

Nephron

Unfiltered blood enters the kidney and flows into millions of tiny capillaries attached to the nephrons.

Artery

Unfiltered blood

Filtered blood

As blood flows through the capillaries, wastes are drawn out of the blood and into the nephron.

Vein

Ureter

Once the blood has been filtered, it flows back out of the kidney.

Urine is collected from all of the nephrons and then flows out of the kidney through the ureter.

Urine

Visualize It!

15 Identify After blood enters the kidneys, name the two paths the fluid takes.

_____
_____
_____
_____
_____
_____
_____
_____

How does the urinary system maintain homeostasis?

Your cells have to maintain a certain level of water and salt in order to function properly. The excretory system works with the endocrine system to help maintain homeostasis. Chemical messengers called *hormones* signal the kidneys to filter more or less water or salt, depending on the levels of water and salt in the body. For example, when you sweat a lot the water content of your blood can drop. When this happens, a hormone is released that signals the kidneys to conserve more water and make less urine. When your blood has too much water, less of the hormone is released. As a result, the nephrons conserve less water, and more urine is produced by the kidneys.

Household or environmental toxins that enter the body through the skin, lungs, or mouth eventually end up in the bloodstream. When the kidneys are damaged, many toxins can accumulate in the blood. Infections can also affect the kidneys. Bacterial infections can occur when bacteria around the opening of the urethra travels up to the bladder and possibly the kidneys.

Active Reading

16 Explain How does exercise affect the balance of salt and water in your body?

_____
_____
_____
_____
_____
_____
_____
_____

Visual Summary

To complete this summary, fill in the blanks with the correct word or phrase. Then, use the answer key to check your answers. You can use this page to review the main concepts of the lesson.

The digestive system breaks down the food you eat into nutrients that provide energy and building materials for cells.

17 The two types of digestion that take place in the mouth are_____. and _____

Digestion and Excretion

The excretory system removes waste from the body.

18 The _____ remove waste from the blood.

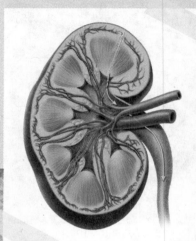

The digestive and excretory sytems work together to process the food that you eat.

19 To process this salad, food is broken down by the _____ _____ and wastes are removed by the _____

Answers:17 mechanical, chemical; 18 kidneys; 19 digestive system, excretory system

20 **Summarize** What types of wastes does the excretory system remove?

Lesson Review

Vocabulary

Fill in the blank with the term that best completes the following sentences.

1 The _____ system helps the body maintain homeostasis by giving it the nutrients it needs to perform different functions.

2 The _____ system eliminates cellular waste through the lungs, skin, and kidneys.

3 The _____ is the name for the hollow muscular organ that stores urine.

Key Concepts

4 Compare What is the difference between mechanical digestion and chemical digestion in the mouth?

_____

_____

_____

5 Describe Starting with the mouth, describe the pathway that food takes through the digestive system.

_____

_____

_____

6 Explain How does the circulatory system interact with the digestive system?

_____

_____

_____

7 Identify Where does urine go after it exits the kidneys?

_____

_____

_____

8 Summarize How do kidneys work with other body systems to maintain homeostasis?

_____

_____

_____

_____

Use the diagram to answer the following question.

9 Apply Identify the organs numbered below.

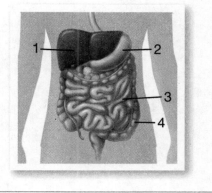

_____

_____

_____

Critical Thinking

10 Relate Why would damaged kidneys affect your health?

_____

_____

_____

_____

11 Infer Suppose a person has a small intestine that has fewer villi than normal. Would the person most likely be overweight or underweight? Explain.

_____

_____

_____

_____

My Notes

The Nervous and Endocrine Systems

ESSENTIAL QUESTION

How do the nervous and endocrine systems work?

By the end of this lesson, you should be able to relate the structures of the nervous and endocrine systems to their functions in the human body.

This sky diver can sense his surroundings and feel the rush of excitement with the help of his nervous and endocrine systems.

✋ Lesson Labs

Quick Labs
- Negative Feedback
- Measuring Reaction Time

Exploration Lab
- Mapping Sensory Receptors

Engage Your Brain

1 Predict Check T or F to show whether you think each statement is true or false.

T	F	
☐	☐	The central nervous system allows us to sense the environment.
☐	☐	The endocrine system functions by sending chemical signals.
☐	☐	The spinal cord is part of the peripheral nervous system.
☐	☐	The endocrine system helps regulate our blood sugar after we eat a meal.

2 Describe Think about a situation that makes you feel very nervous or anxious. Describe how this makes you feel inside. What do you think is going on in your body?

_____

_____

_____

_____

_____

Active Reading

3 Apply You can often understand the meaning of a word if you use it in a sentence. Use the following definition to write your own sentence that has the word *gland*.

Definition
<u>gland</u>: a group of cells that make special chemicals for the body

gland:

_____

_____

_____

_____

Vocabulary Terms

- nervous system
- brain
- spinal cord
- neuron
- axon
- dendrite
- endocrine system
- hormone
- gland

4 Apply As you learn the definition of each vocabulary term in this lesson, create your own definition or sketch to help you remember the meaning of the term.

Brainiac!

What is the function of the nervous system?

The **nervous system** is made of the structures that control the actions and reactions of the body in response to stimuli from the environment. Your nervous system has two parts: the central nervous system (CNS) and the peripheral (puh•RIFF•uh•rahl) nervous system (PNS).

The CNS Processes Information

The brain and the spinal cord make up the CNS. The **brain** is the body's central command organ. It constantly receives impulses from all over the body. Your **spinal cord** allows your brain to communicate with the rest of your body. Your nervous system is mostly made up of specialized cells that send and receive electrical signals.

The PNS Connects the CNS to Muscles and Organs

Your PNS connects your CNS to the rest of your body. The PNS has two main parts—the sensory part and the motor part. Many processes that the brain controls happen automatically—you have no control over them. These processes are called *involuntary*. For example, you could not stop your heart from beating even if you tried. However, some of the actions of your brain you can control—these are *voluntary*. Moving your arm is a voluntary action.

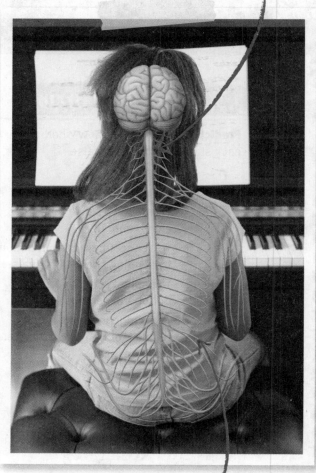

The CNS is shown in yellow.

The PNS is shown in green.

Parts of the CNS
brain
and _spinal cord_

The CNS and PNS are both made of _brain_

Parts of the PNS
motor part
and _sensory part_

5 Compare Fill in the Venn diagram to compare and contrast the structure of the CNS and the PNS.

What are the parts of the CNS?

The CNS is made up of the brain and the spinal cord.

The Brain

The three main areas of the brain are the cerebrum, the cerebellum, and the brain stem. The largest part of the brain is the cerebrum. The cerebrum is where you think and problem-solve, and where most of your memories are stored. It controls voluntary movements and allows you to sense touch, light, sound, odors, taste, pain, heat, and cold. The second largest part of your brain is the cerebellum. It processes information from your body. This allows the brain to keep track of your body's position and coordinate movements. The brain stem connects your brain to your spinal cord. The medulla is part of the brain stem. It controls involuntary processes, such as blood pressure, body temperature, heart rate, and involuntary breathing.

6 Identify List a function of each part of the brain shown here.

Cerebrum
Controls voluntary movements.

Cerebellum
• processes info
• Allows brain to keep track of the body's position and movements.

Brain stem
Connects the brain to the spinal cord.

The Spinal Cord

The spinal cord is made of bundles of nerves. A *nerve* is a collection of nerve cell extensions bundled together with blood vessels and connective tissue. Nerves are everywhere in your body. The spinal cord is surrounded by protective bones called *vertebrae*.

Special cells in your skin and muscles carry sensory information to the spinal cord. The spinal cord carries these impulses to the brain. The brain interprets these impulses as warmth, pain, or other sensations and sends information back to the spinal cord. Different cells in the spinal cord then send impulses to the rest of the body to create a response.

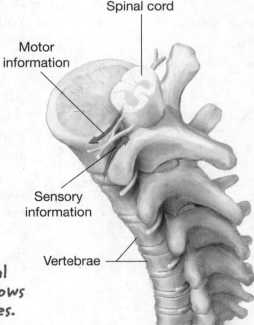

Spinal cord

Motor information

Sensory information

Vertebrae

Sensory information (red) flows in from the environment to the spinal cord. Motor information (blue) flows out from the spinal cord to muscles.

You've Got Nerves!

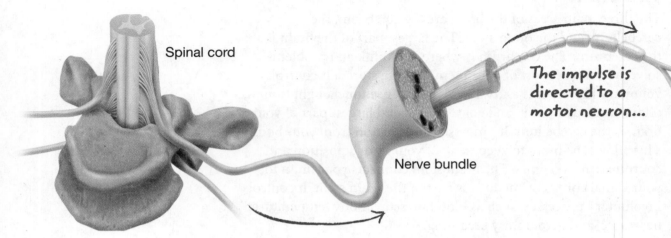

Spinal cord

Nerve bundle

The impulse is directed to a motor neuron...

If you notice that your shoe is untied, your brain interprets this information and sends an impulse down the spinal cord.

How do signals move through the nervous system?

Your nervous system works by receiving information from the environment and translating that information into electrical signals. Those electrical signals are sent from the brain to the rest of the body by special cells called *neurons*. A **neuron** is a cell that moves messages in the form of fast-moving electrical energy. These electrical messages are called *impulses*.

Signals move through the central and peripheral nervous systems with the help of glial (GLEE•uhl) cells. Glial cells do not transmit nerve impulses, but they protect and support neurons. Without glial cells, neurons would not work properly. Your brain has about 100 billion neurons, but there are about 10 to 50 times more glial cells in your brain.

Through Sensory and Motor Neurons

Neurons carry information from the body to the brain, and carry instructions from the brain back to the rest of the body. The two groups of neurons are sensory neurons and motor neurons.

Sensory neurons gather information from in and around your body. They then move this information to the brain. Motor neurons move impulses from the brain and spinal cord to other parts of the body. For example, when you are hot, motor neurons move messages from your brain to your sweat glands to tell the sweat glands to make sweat. Sweating cools your body.

> **Active Reading**
>
> **7 Identify** As you read, underline the special types of neurons that receive and send messages.

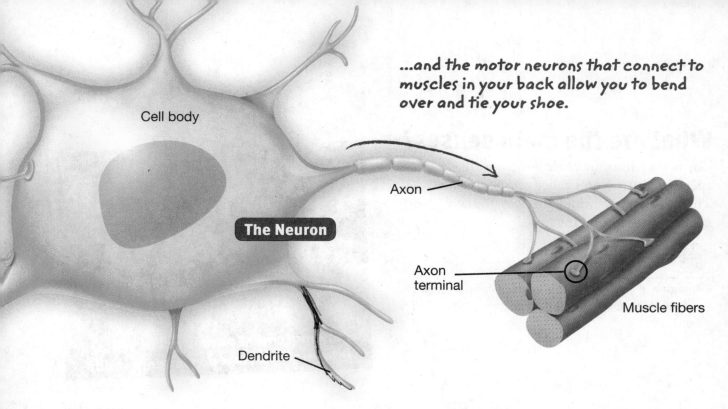

Cell body

The Neuron

...and the motor neurons that connect to muscles in your back allow you to bend over and tie your shoe.

Axon

Axon terminal

Muscle fibers

Dendrite

What are the parts of a neuron?

A neuron is made up of a large region called the *cell body,* a long extension called the *axon,* and short branches called *dendrites.* At the end of the axon is the *axon terminal.*

Like other cells, a neuron's cell body has a nucleus and organelles. But neurons have other structures that allow them to communicate with other cells. A **dendrite** (DEHN•dryt) is a usually short, branched extension of the cell body. A neuron may have one, two, or many dendrites. Neurons with many dendrites can receive impulses from thousands of cells at a time. The cell body gathers information from the dendrites and creates an impulse.

Impulses are carried away from the cell body by extensions of the neuron, called an **axon**. A neuron has only one axon, and they can be very short or quite long. Some long axons extend almost 1 m from your lower back to your toes! Impulses move in one direction along the axon.

At the end of an axon is the axon terminal, where a signal is changed from an electrical signal to a chemical signal. This chemical signal, called a *neurotransmitter,* is released into the gap between the neuron and other cells.

 **Visualize It!**

8 Apply In the boxes below, fill in the appropriate neuron parts, structures, or functions.

NEURON PART	STRUCTURE	FUNCTION
Cell body	region containing nucleus and organelles	contains organells and nucleus
dendrite	branches of the cell body	gathers information from other cells
Axon	extention of a neuron	sends impulse away from cell body
axon terminal	end of an axon	changes electrical signal to chemical signal

That Makes Sense!

What are the main senses?

The body senses the environment with specialized structures called *sensory organs*. These structures include the eyes, the skin, the ears, the mouth, and the nose.

9 Imagine If you were at this amusement park, what do you think you would see, hear, smell, taste, and feel?

_____

_____

An amusement park is full of sensory information! How do we sense it all?

Sight

Your eye allows you to see the size, shape, motion, and color of objects around you. The front of the eye is covered by a clear membrane called the *cornea*. Light from an object passes through an opening called the *pupil*. Light hits the eye's lens, an oval-shaped piece of clear, curved material. Eye muscles change the shape of the lens to focus light onto the retina. The *retina* (RET•nuh) is a layer of light-sensitive photoreceptor cells that change light into electrical impulses. These cells, called *rods* and *cones,* generate nerve impulses that are sent to the brain.

Rays form an upside-down image on the retina at the back of the eye. This image is translated by the brain.

Lens

Cornea

Retina

Pupil

Light enters the eye through the lens. Light rays are bent by the cornea.

Visualize It!

10 Identify What part of the eye focuses light on to the retina?

pupil
_____

Touch

You feel a tap on your shoulder. The tap produces impulses in sensory receptors on your shoulder. These impulses travel to your brain. Once the impulses reach your brain, they create an awareness called a *sensation*. In this case, the sensation is that of your shoulder being touched. The skin has different kinds of receptors that detect pressure, temperature, pain, and vibration.

Hearing

Ears pick up sound wave vibrations. These sound waves push air particles, creating a wave of sound energy. The sensory cells of your ears turn sound waves into electrical impulses. These electrical impulses then travel to your brain. Each ear has an outer, a middle, and an inner portion. Sound waves reaching the outer ear are funneled toward the middle ear. There, the waves make the eardrum vibrate. The *eardrum* is a thin membrane separating the outer ear from the middle ear. The vibrating eardrum makes three tiny bones in the middle ear vibrate. The last of these bones vibrates against the *cochlea* (KOH•klee•uh), a fluid-filled organ of the inner ear. Inside the cochlea, the vibrations make waves in the fluid. Sensory receptors called *hair cells* move about in the fluid. Movement of the hair cells causes neurons in the cochlea to send electrical impulses. These impulses travel to the brain via the auditory nerve and are interpreted as sound.

The ears also help you maintain balance. Special fluid-filled canals in the inner ear are filled with hair cells that respond to changes in head orientation. These hair cells then send signals to the brain about the position of the head with respect to gravity.

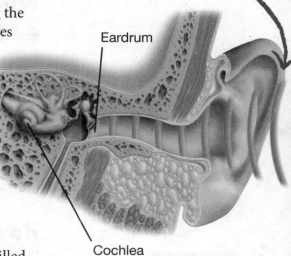

Sound waves enter the ear and cause the eardrum to vibrate. The vibrations are translated by receptors.

Eardrum

Cochlea

Taste

Your tongue is covered with taste buds. These taste buds contain clusters of *taste cells* that respond to signals in dissolved molecules in food. Taste cells react to five basic tastes: sweet, sour, salty, bitter, and savory. Your sense of taste can protect you from eating something that could be harmful.

Smell

The nose is your sense organ for smell. Receptors for smell are located in the upper part of your nasal cavity. Sensory receptors called *olfactory cells* react to chemicals in the air. These molecules dissolve in the moist lining of the nasal cavity and trigger an impulse in the receptors. The nerve impulses are sent to the brain, where they are interpreted as an odor. Your senses of taste and smell work together to allow you to taste a variety of food flavors. Both senses detect chemical cues in the environment.

Olfactory cells

Molecules in the air enter your nose. There, they bind to receptors in the top of your nasal cavity.

11 Apply If you have a cold that causes congestion in your sinuses, how might that affect your sense of smell?

<u>You might not be able to smell</u>
<u>that well with your nose clogged</u>

Keep Your Cool!

What is the function of the endocrine system?

Your **endocrine system** controls body functions and helps maintain homeostasis by using hormones. A **hormone** is a chemical messenger made in one cell or tissue that causes a change in another cell or tissue in a different part of the body. Hormones are produced by endocrine glands or tissues. A **gland** is a group of cells that make special chemicals for your body. Unlike direct signals of the nervous system, the signals sent by the endocrine system are indirect because they cycle through the whole body.

How do hormones work?

Hormones travel through the bloodstream. They travel from the endocrine gland where they are made and can reach every cell in the body. However, hormones affect only the cells that have specific _receptors_. Each hormone has its own receptor and affects only cells that have that receptor. These cells are called _target cells_. Many cells throughout the body have the same receptors, so hormones are able to perform many functions at the same time in different cells.

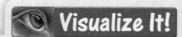
Active Reading

12 Identify As you read, underline the structure which allows hormones to affect only certain cells.

Visualize It!

13 Apply Explain the difference between an endocrine cell and a target cell.

The endocrine cell makes hormones the target cell collects those hormones.

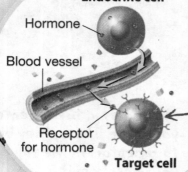

- **Endocrine cell**
- Hormone
- Blood vessel
- Receptor for hormone
- **Target cell**

When you are surprised, a hormone called adrenaline makes you more alert.

Hormones are released from an endocrine cell and travel through the bloodstream to bind to a receptor on a target cell. Sometimes a target cell is very far away!

What glands make up the endocrine system?

Your body has several endocrine glands or tissues that make up the endocrine system.

- Your pituitary gland is very important because it secretes hormones that affect other glands. It also stimulates growth and sexual development.
- The hypothalamus is a gland in the brain that controls the release of hormones from the pituitary gland.
- The pineal gland, also in the brain, produces hormones essential in the control of sleep, aging, reproduction, and body temperature.
- Hormones from the thyroid control your metabolism.
- The parathyroid gland controls calcium levels in the blood.
- Hormones made in the reproductive organs (ovaries or testes) control reproduction.
- Other endocrine glands include the pancreas and adrenal glands. The pancreas regulates blood sugar levels and the adrenal glands control the body's fight or flight response in dangerous situations.

These are the major endocrine glands. They regulate important body functions.

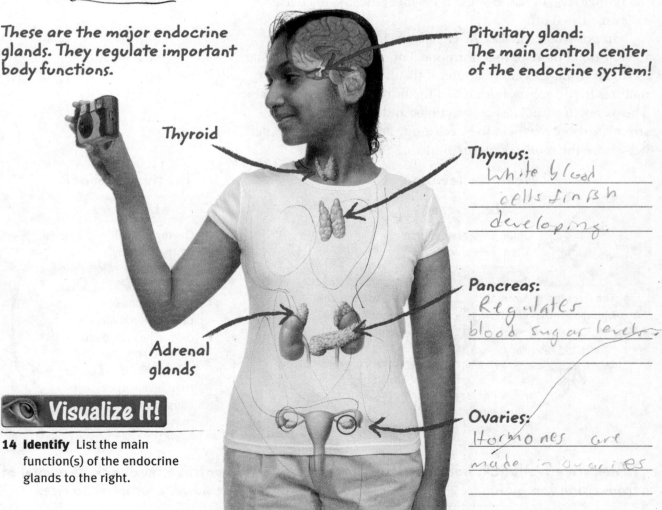

Thyroid

Adrenal glands

Pituitary gland: The main control center of the endocrine system!

Thymus:
White blood cells finish developing.

Pancreas:
Regulates blood sugar levels.

Ovaries:
Hormones are made in ovaries

Visualize It!

14 Identify List the main function(s) of the endocrine glands to the right.

Feed◄Back

How are hormone levels controlled?

The endocrine system keeps the body's internal environment in homeostasis. It does this by increasing or decreasing the amount of hormones in the bloodstream, some of which may have opposite effects on body cells. Such a process is called a feedback mechanism. A *feedback mechanism* is a cycle of events in which information from one step controls or affects a previous step.

By Feedback Mechanisms

There are two types of feedback, positive and negative. In negative feedback, the effects of a hormone in the body cause the release of that hormone to be turned down. For example, when you eat food, your blood sugar levels go up. Insulin is released and blood sugar levels are lowered. Once this happens, the lower blood sugar levels tell the pancreas to stop releasing insulin. In other words, when the proper level of blood sugar is reached, the insulin-releasing cells are turned off.

In positive feedback, the effects of a hormone stimulate the release of more of that hormone. For example, the hormone oxytocin stimulates contractions of the uterus. When a fetus matures in the uterus, both it and the mother produce oxytocin. The oxytocin stimulates contractions, and these contractions stimulate more oxytocin to be released. The contractions expel a baby from the mother's uterus at birth.

15 Compare Describe the difference between negative and positive feedback.

In negative feedback, hormone levels are kept from going too high, but in positive feedback the hormones continue to rise.

Negative Feedback

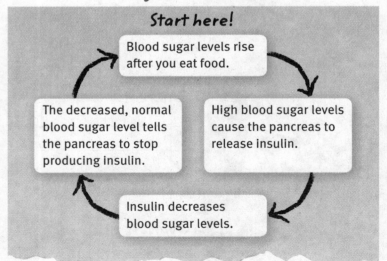

Start here!

Blood sugar levels rise after you eat food.

High blood sugar levels cause the pancreas to release insulin.

Insulin decreases blood sugar levels.

The decreased, normal blood sugar level tells the pancreas to stop producing insulin.

In negative feedback, hormone levels are kept from rising too high.

Positive Feedback

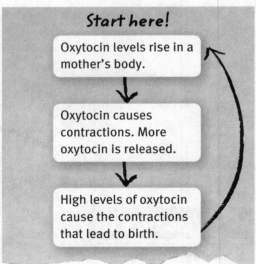

Start here!

Oxytocin levels rise in a mother's body.

Oxytocin causes contractions. More oxytocin is released.

High levels of oxytocin cause the contractions that lead to birth.

In positive feedback, the level of hormones continues to rise.

What are disorders of the endocrine and nervous systems?

The endocrine system and nervous system are both responsible for sending messages around our bodies. If a problem developed with one or more of these systems, other systems of the body would need to adjust to compensate for this loss.

Hormone Imbalances

Disorders of the endocrine system occur when an endocrine gland makes too much or not enough of a hormone. For example, a person whose pancreas does not make enough insulin has a condition called type 1 diabetes. This condition causes an imbalance of the blood sugar. A person who has diabetes may need daily injections of insulin to keep blood sugar levels within safe limits. Some patients receive their insulin automatically from a small pump worn next to the body. New technology allows people with type 1 diabetes to intake insulin using an inhaler.

17 Describe How does the insulin pump help a person with type 1 diabetes maintain homeostasis?

The body does not normally produce a lot of insulin when someone has diabetes, so a pump helps.

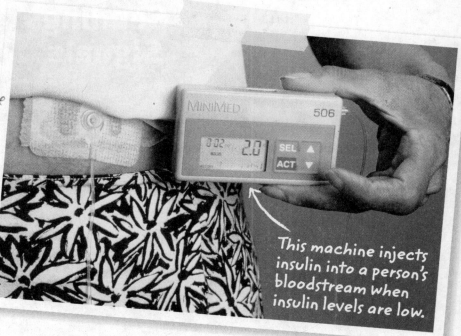

This machine injects insulin into a person's bloodstream when insulin levels are low.

Nerve Damage

Disorders of the nervous system include Parkinson's disease, multiple sclerosis, and spinal cord injury. In Parkinson's disease, the cells that control movement are damaged. Multiple sclerosis affects the brain's ability to send signals to the rest of the body.

A spinal cord injury may block information to and from the brain. For example, impulses coming from the feet and legs may be blocked. People with such an injury cannot sense pain in their legs. The person would also not be able to move his or her legs, because impulses from the brain could not get past the injury site.

Visual Summary

To complete this summary, fill in the blank to answer the question. Then, use the key below to check your answers. You can use this page to review the main concepts of the lesson.

The nervous system gathers information and responds by sending electrical signals.

18 Nerve cells called _____ carry electrical messages called _____

The endocrine system controls conditions in your body by sending chemical messages.

19 Hormones have specific actions by attaching to _receptors_ on target cells.

Sending Signals

Hormones are controlled by feedback mechanisms.

20 _Negative_ feedback is when higher levels of a hormone turn off the production of that hormone.

Negative Feedback
Start here!

Blood sugar levels rise after you eat food.

High blood sugar cause the pancreas to release insulin.

Insulin decreases blood sugar levels.

The decreased, normal blood sugar level tells the pancreas to stop producing insulin.

Answers: 18 neurons, impulses; 19 receptors; 20 Negative

21 **Apply** Describe how both your nervous and endocrine systems would be involved if you walked into a surprise party and were truly surprised.

Lesson Review

Vocabulary

Use a term from the section to complete each sentence below.

1 The _____ is made up of the brain and spinal cord.

2 Glands in the _endocrine cell_ send messages to target cells.

3 Use *gland* and *hormone* in the same sentence.

A hormones is produced by an endocrine glands.

4 Use *hormone* and *feedback mechanism* in the same sentence.

_____

_____

_____

Key Concepts

5 Identify Describe the function of the PNS and the CNS.

_____

_____

_____

_____

6 Apply What are the parts of a neuron?

_____

_____

_____

_____

7 Identify How are the messages of the endocrine system moved around the body?

The messages are moved around on the blood stream

_____

_____

8 Identify What is the main sense organ for each of the five senses?

_____

_____

_____

_____

Critical Thinking

The images below show how an eye responds to different light levels. Use the image to answer the following question.

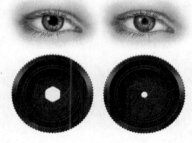

9 Interpret The pupil opens and closes automatically in response to light. What part of your nervous system controls this response?

_____

_____

10 Infer Explain whether this is a voluntary or involuntary action.

_____

_____

_____

_____

11 Predict How would your body be affected if your pituitary gland was not working properly?

_____

_____

_____

_____

_____

My Notes

Engineering Design Process

Skills
✔ **Identify a need**
Conduct research
✔ **Brainstorm solutions**
✔ **Select a solution**
Build a prototype
Test and evaluate
Redesign to improve
✔ **Communicate results**

Objectives
• Identify a market need.
• Design an assistive device.
• Draw a prototype.

Designing a Device

The human body is an amazing machine, but sometimes it can use a little help. *Assistive devices* are devices that are designed for use by people with disabilities. Creating assistive devices to meet the needs of targeted groups of individuals is known as market needs. Some of these devices are integrated with the body, some are worn on the body, and some are tools that people use. Major categories of assistive devices include communication devices, hygiene (HY•jeen) or medication aids, vision aids, hearing aids, mobility aids, and eating aids. These devices include wheelchairs or grab bars, pacemakers, and internal insulin (IN•suh•lin) pumps. Also, hand railings help people climb stairs, shower handles help people get in and out of the shower, and sidewalk bumps help the visually impaired. These are all examples of ways that engineering is applied to life science.

1 Describe Look at the photo on this page. What examples of assistive devices do you see?

_____

_____

_____

We Can All Use a Little Help

Some of the better-known assistive devices, such as wheelchairs or crutches, help with injuries or disabilities. For example, if you break your leg, your doctor will likely give you crutches to help you to get around while you heal. But many assistive or adaptive devices just simplify daily tasks. Small tools such as buttonhooks help people button their shirts, long-handled shoehorns make it easier to put on shoes, and special utensils make eating easier. Many adaptive devices are also integrated into your everyday environment. For example, some people wear glasses or contact lenses to improve their vision or get hearing aids to help their hearing.

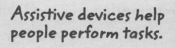
Assistive devices help people perform tasks.

2 Explain For one of the devices shown above, state what the assistive device is and how it is helpful.

_____

_____

_____

_____

 You Try It! ⟶

Now it's your turn to design an assistive device.

✋ You Try It!

Now it's your turn to design a realistic assistive device that people need. You will think about what people might need to do, decide which is the most promising idea, draw a prototype of your device, and present your idea to your class.

① Identify a Need

A Imagine a need for each category of assistive device given below. Think of people you know of who a need an assistive device for a daily task. Consider what an older person might need, or someone who is physically disabled.

Grasping	Hygiene	Communication	Mobility	Eating

B To find which idea has the biggest potential impact, make a Pugh chart from the following model. Rank each idea from 1 to 10, with 10 indicating the best fit with the criterion indicated in the criteria column. Find the total for each column.

Criteria	Grasping	Hygiene	Communication	Mobility	Eating
Frequency of use 1 = not often 10 = very often					
Number of users 1 = few 10 = many					
Product lifetime 1 = long 10 = short					
Total					

② Brainstorm Solutions

In your group, brainstorm ideas for assistive devices that would address the biggest market identified in your Pugh chart.

_____

_____

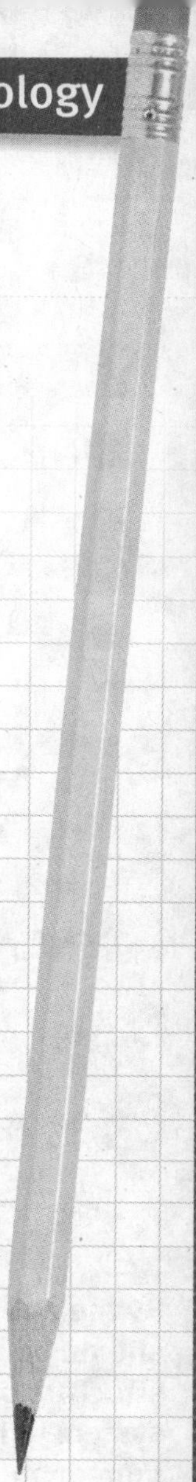

③ Select a Solution

With the members of your group, decide on the best idea from your brainstorming session. Then, in the space below, draw a prototype of your chosen idea, and list the materials needed to make it. Be as detailed as possible (use extra paper if necessary).

④ Communicate Results

Summarize the information about your device. Describe the need that the device addresses, who the users would be, the device itself and how it works, and any other things you think are important to explain your device to another person. Then, as a group, use the summary information to create a poster of your idea to present to the class.

_____

_____

_____

_____

_____

The Reproductive System

ESSENTIAL QUESTION

How does your reproductive system work?

By the end of this lesson, you should be able to relate the structure of the reproductive system to its function in the human body.

Many pregnant women do exercises such as yoga or other stretches to stay healthy as their baby develops.

Engage Your Brain

1 Predict Have you met a woman who was pregnant? Write a short answer describing what type of development you think is going on inside a pregnant woman.

_____

_____

_____

_____

_____

_____

_____

2 Apply Name five things that have changed about you from your fifth to your tenth birthday.

_____

_____

_____

_____

_____

_____

Active Reading

3 Explain You may be familiar with the eggs that farmers collect from chickens. Females of many species, including humans, produce eggs as part of the reproductive cycle. How do you think a human egg is similar to a chicken egg? How do you think they are different?

_____

_____

_____

_____

_____

Vocabulary Terms

- sperm
- testes
- penis
- egg
- ovary
- uterus
- vagina
- embryo
- placenta
- umbilical cord
- fetus

4 Apply As you learn the definition of each vocabulary term in this lesson, create your own definition or sketch to help you remember the meaning of the term.

Reproduction

What are the main functions of the male reproductive system?

The male reproductive system functions to produce sperm and deliver sperm to the female reproductive system. **Sperm** are the male cells that are used for reproduction. Each sperm cell carries 23 chromosomes, half of the chromosomes of other body cells. The male reproductive system also produces hormones.

Hormones are chemical messengers that control many important body functions such as growth, development, and sex-cell production. The **testes** (singular, *testis*) are the main organs of the male reproductive system. These organs produce *testosterone*, the male sex hormone. Testosterone causes male characteristics to develop, such as facial hair and a deep voice.

The testes also make sperm. After sperm mature, they are stored in the *epididymis* (EH•puh•DIH•duh•miss). They leave the epididymis through a tube called the *vas deferens* and mix with fluids from several glands. This mixture of sperm and fluids is called *semen*. To leave the body, semen passes through the *urethra*, the tube that runs through the penis. The **penis** is the organ that delivers semen into the female reproductive system.

Active Reading

5 Identify As you read, underline the functions of the main hormones in the male and female reproductive systems.

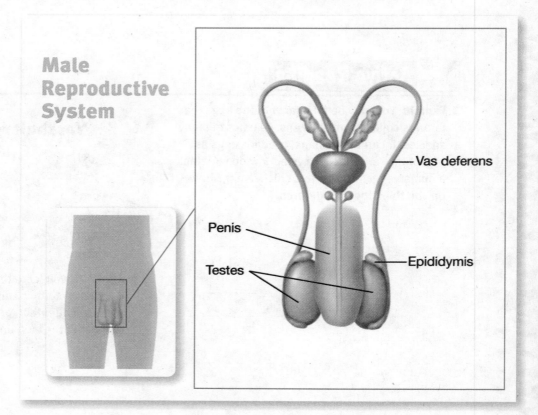

Male Reproductive System

Vas deferens

Penis

Epididymis

Testes

What are the main functions of the female reproductive system?

The female reproductive system produces hormones and eggs, and provides a place to nourish a developing human. An **egg** is the female sex cell. Like sperm, egg cells have 23 chromosomes, only half the number of other body cells.

The female reproductive system produces the sex hormones *estrogen* and *progesterone*. These hormones control the development of female characteristics, such as breasts and wider hips. They also regulate the development and release of eggs, and they prepare the body for pregnancy.

An **ovary** is the reproductive organ that produces eggs. At sexual maturity, females have hundreds of thousands of immature eggs in their ovaries. Like sperm, eggs are produced through the process of meiosis. During a female's lifetime, usually about 400 of her eggs will mature and be released from the ovaries.

Female Reproductive System

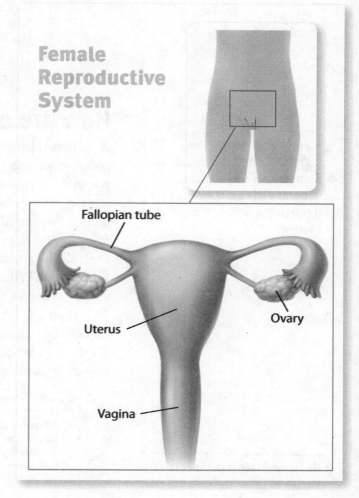

Fallopian tube

Uterus

Ovary

Vagina

---

6 Summarize Fill in the chart below to summarize the structures of the male and female reproductive systems.

Sex	Sex cell	Organ that produces sex cell	Other reproductive organs
Male	Sperm	Testes	Penis
Female	egg	Ovary	Vagina

---

7 Contrast What makes sperm cells and egg cells different from almost all other types of body cells?

Sperm and egg cells have 23 chromosomes (half the amount of chromosomes in other body cells)

Fertile ground

How are eggs released?

A woman's reproductive system goes through changes that produce an egg, release the egg, and prepare the body for pregnancy. These changes are called the *menstrual cycle* and usually take about one month. About halfway through the cycle, an egg is released from the ovary. The egg travels through the *fallopian tube*, a pair of tubes that connect each ovary to the uterus. The **uterus** is the organ in which a fertilized egg develops into a baby. When a baby is born, it passes through the **vagina**, the canal between the uterus and the outside of the body.

If an egg is not fertilized, it is shed with the lining of the uterus. The monthly discharge of blood and tissue from the uterus is called *menstruation*. When menstruation ends, the lining of the uterus thickens and the cycle begins again.

🖊 **Active Reading**

8 Summarize As you read, underline the path an egg takes through the female reproductive system.

9 Number Place a number in the circles to order the steps of the menstrual cycle.

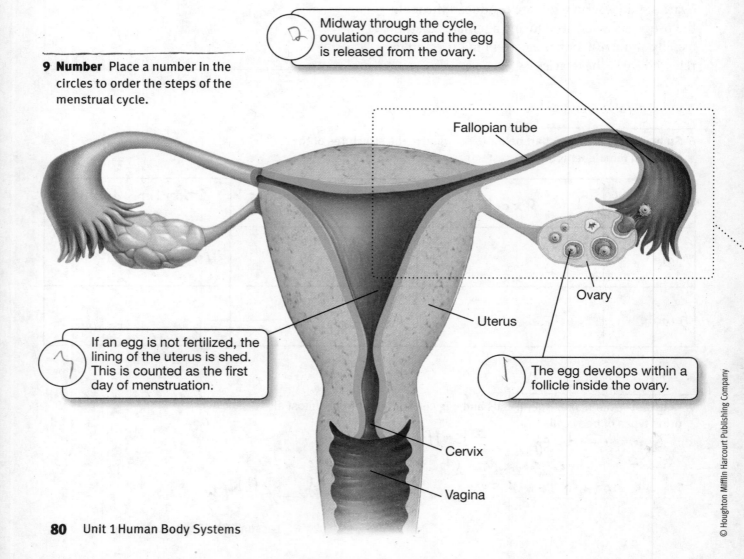

Midway through the cycle, ovulation occurs and the egg is released from the ovary.

Fallopian tube

Ovary

Uterus

If an egg is not fertilized, the lining of the uterus is shed. This is counted as the first day of menstruation.

The egg develops within a follicle inside the ovary.

Cervix

Vagina

How are eggs fertilized?

When sperm enter the female reproductive system, a few hundred make it through the uterus into a fallopian tube. There, the sperm release enzymes that help dissolve the egg's outer covering.

When a sperm enters an egg, the egg's membrane changes to stop other sperm from entering. During fertilization, the egg and sperm combine to form one cell. Once cell division occurs, the fertilized egg becomes an **embryo**. The genetic material from the father and the mother combine and a unique individual begins to develop. Usually, only one sperm gets through the outer covering of the egg. If more than one sperm enter the egg, multiple identical embryos can form. After fertilization, the embryo travels from the fallopian tube to the uterus over five to six days, and attaches to the thickened and nutrient-rich lining of the uterus.

 Inquiry

10 Infer Sometimes more than one egg is released at a time. What do you think would happen if two eggs were released and both were fertilized? Explain your answer.

There would be 2 babies, but not twins.

11 Summarize Determine what happens if an egg is fertilized and if it is not fertilized, and fill in both of the boxes below.

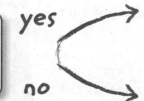

Was the egg fertilized?

yes →

no →

The egg is shed with the lining of the uterus and with blood and tissue exits through the vagina

Steps of Fertilization

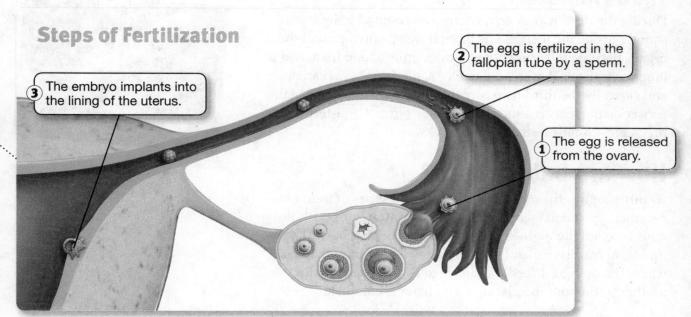

③ The embryo implants into the lining of the uterus.

② The egg is fertilized in the fallopian tube by a sperm.

① The egg is released from the ovary.

Happy Birthday!

What are the stages of pregnancy?

A normal pregnancy lasts about nine months. These nine months are broken down into three 3-month periods, called *trimesters*.

Active Reading **12 Identify** Underline three things that take place during each trimester.

First Trimester

Soon after implantation, the placenta begins to grow. The **placenta** is a network of blood vessels that provides the embryo with oxygen and nutrients from the mother's blood and carries away wastes. The embryo is surrounded by the *amnion,* a sac filled with fluid that protects the embryo. The embryo connects to the placenta by the **umbilical cord**. After week 10, the embryo is called a **fetus**. Many organs such as the heart, liver and brain form. Arms and legs as well as fingers and toes also form during this trimester.

Second Trimester

During the second trimester, joints and bones start to form. The fetus's muscles grow stronger. As a result, the fetus can make a fist and begins to move. The fetus triples its size within a month and its brain begins to grow rapidly. Eventually, the fetus can make faces. The fetus starts to make movements the mother can feel. Toward the end of the trimester, the fetus can breathe and swallow.

Third Trimester

During the third trimester, the fetus can respond to light and sound outside the uterus. The brain develops further, and the organs become fully functional. Bones grow and harden, and the lungs completely develop. By week 32, the fetus's eyes can open and close. By the third trimester the fetus can also dream. After 36 weeks, the fetus is almost ready to be born. A full-term pregnancy usually lasts about 40 weeks.

How are babies born?

As birth begins, the mother's uterus starts a series of muscular contractions called *labor.* Usually, these contractions push the fetus through the mother's vagina, and the baby is born. The umbilical cord is tied and cut. All that will remain of the place where the umbilical cord was attached is the navel. Finally, the mother pushes out the placenta, and labor is complete.

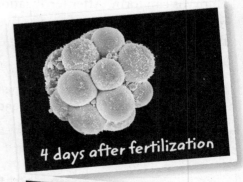

4 days after fertilization

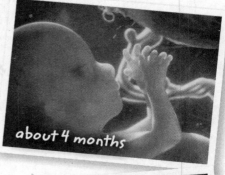

about 4 months

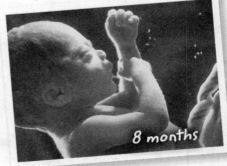

8 months

What changes occur during infancy and childhood?

Development during infancy and childhood includes gaining control of skeletal muscles and learning to speak. Generally, infancy is the stage from birth to age 2. During infancy, babies grow quickly and baby teeth appear. The nervous system develops, and babies become more coordinated and start to walk. Many babies begin to say words by age 1. During this time, the body is growing rapidly. Childhood lasts from age 2 to puberty. Baby teeth are replaced by permanent teeth. Children learn to speak fluently and their muscles become more coordinated, allowing them to run, jump, and perform other activities.

What changes occur during adolescence and adulthood?

The stage from puberty to adulthood is *adolescence*. During adolescence, a person's reproductive system becomes mature. In most boys, puberty takes place between the ages of 9 and 16. During this time, the young male's body becomes more muscular, his voice becomes deeper, and body and facial hair appear. In most girls, puberty takes place between the ages of 9 and 15. During this time, the amount of fat in the hips and thighs increases, the breasts enlarge, body hair appears, and menstruation begins.

During adulthood, a person reaches physical and emotional maturity. A person is considered a young adult from about age 20 to age 40. Beginning around age 30, changes associated with aging begin. The aging process continues into middle age (between 40 and 65 years old). During this time, hair may turn gray, athletic abilities will decline, and skin may wrinkle. A person more than 65 years old is considered an older adult. Exercising and eating well-balanced diets help people stay healthy as they grow older.

Do the Math

Everyone grows as they age, but does the amount you grow change as you get older?

Sample Problem

To calculate growth rate, divide the difference in height by the difference in age. For example, the growth rate between the ages of one and five for the girl shown below is:

$(102 \text{ cm} - 71 \text{ cm}) \div (5 \text{ years} - 1 \text{ year}) = 8 \text{ cm/year}$

You Try It

13 Calculate Determine the growth rate for the girl between the ages of 14 and 19. Is the amount of growth greater between ages 1 and 5 or between ages 14 and 19?

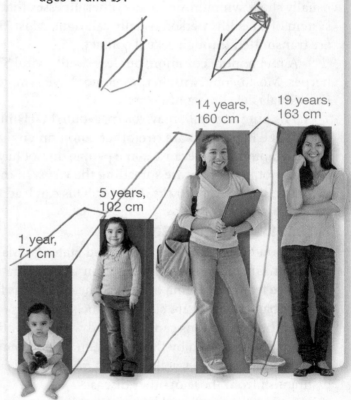

14 years, 160 cm

19 years, 163 cm

5 years, 102 cm

1 year, 71 cm

Think Outside the Book

14 Research Learning a new language can be easier for young children. This phenomenon is known as a "critical period." Research critical periods for language and write a short report describing what you learned.

© Houghton Mifflin Harcourt Publishing Company • Image Credits: (1 yr.) ©Jupiterimages/Comstock Images/Getty Images; (5 yrs.) ©Gregory Costanzo/Digital Vision/Getty Images; (14 yrs.) ©Blend Images/Alamy; (19 yrs.) ©Tetra Images/Getty Images

Infections

What causes STIs?

Sexually transmitted infections (STIs) are infections that are passed from one person to another during sexual contact. STIs can be caused by viruses, bacteria, or parasites.

Active Reading **15 Identify** As you read, underline the symptoms of each STI listed below.

Viruses

Acquired immunodeficiency syndrome (AIDS) is caused by the human immunodeficiency virus (HIV). This virus infects and destroys immune system cells. As a result, people with AIDS usually show symptoms of many other illnesses that the immune system of a healthy person usually can fight. Most HIV infections are transmitted through sexual contact.

A much more common, but less deadly, viral STI is genital herpes. Most people with herpes do not have symptoms, but some individuals develop painful sores.

The human papillomavirus (paa•puh•LOH•muh•vy•russ) (HPV) and hepatitis B are two other common viral STIs that are often symptomless. Because some people do not have symptoms, they do not know they are spreading the virus. In the case of hepatitis B, the virus attacks the liver. This can lead to death.

Bacteria and Parasites

A common bacterial STI in the United States is chlamydia. Symptoms include a burning sensation when urinating or a discharge from the vagina or penis. The symptoms for gonorrhea, another bacterial STI, are similar to the symptoms of chlamydia. Both of these infections can be treated with antibiotics. Another STI, syphilis, is caused by the bacterium *Treponema pallidum*. Its symptoms, such as swollen glands, rash and fever, are hard to distinguish from those of other diseases.

Some STIs are caused by parasites. For example, the STI trichomoniasis is caused by the protozoan *Trichomonas vaginalis*. It is the most common curable STI for young women. Symptoms are more common in women and may include a genital discharge and pain during urination. Another parasitic STI is a pubic lice infestation. Pubic lice are tiny insects that feed on blood. The most common symptom of a pubic lice infection is genital itching.

16 Label For each photo below, label the type of infection as a virus, a bacterium, or a parasite.

Chlamydia cell

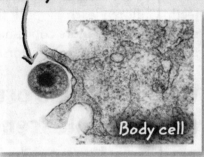

Body cell

Herpes-infected immune cells

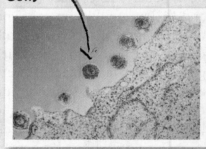

Syphilis cell

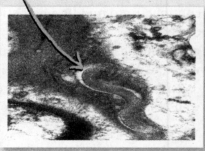

Seeing Double

HEALTH WATCH

Multiple births occur when two or more babies are carried during the same pregnancy. In humans, the most common type of multiple births occurs when the mother gives birth to two children, or twins. About 3% of all births in the United States result in twins.

Fraternal Siblings

Fraternal siblings form when two sperm fertilize two or more separate eggs. Fraternal siblings can be the same gender or different genders and are as different genetically as any ordinary siblings.

Identical Twins

Identical twins form when a single sperm fertilizes a single egg. The developing embryo then divides in two. Identical twins are always the same gender and are genetically identical.

Triplets

While twinning is the most common type of multiple birth, other multiples still occur. About 0.1% of all births are triplets.

Extend

Inquiry

17 Infer Based on how identical twins form, infer how identical triplets could develop.

18 Research Describe some shared behavioral traits or language between twins and give an example.

19 Create Illustrate how fertilized eggs develop into fraternal triplets. You may choose to make a poster, make a model, or write a short story.

Visual Summary

To complete this summary, circle the correct word. Then, use the key below to check your answers. You can use this page to review the main concepts of the lesson.

The male reproductive system makes hormones and sperm cells.

20 Sperm are produced in the penis / ~~testes~~.

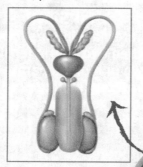

The female reproductive system makes hormones and egg cells, and protects a developing baby if fertilization occurs.

21 Eggs are produced in the ~~ovary~~ / vagina.

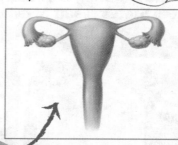

Reproduction and Development

A baby goes through many changes as it develops into an adult.

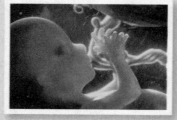

22 During pregnancy, a growing baby gets oxygen and nourishment from an organ called the embryo / ~~placenta~~.

Sexually transmitted infections (STIs) are caused by viruses, bacteria, and parasites.

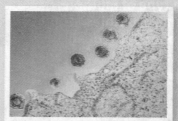

23 STIs are spread through the air / ~~sexual contact~~.

Answers: 20 testes; 21 ovary; 22 placenta; 23 sexual contact

24 **Applying Concepts** Why does the egg's covering change after a sperm has entered the egg?

Lesson Review

Vocabulary

1 Use *uterus* and *vagina* in the same sentence.

The baby develops in the uterus then when it is ready, comes out of the vagina during birth.

2 Use *sperm* and *egg* in the same sentence.

To start the fertilization process, the sperm "swim" to the egg where they get fused together.

Key Concepts

3 Compare Compare the functions of the male and female reproductive systems.

The male reproductive system produces sperm which is delivered (through the penis) into the female reproductive reproductive system.

4 Summarize Summarize the processes of fertilization and implantation.

5 Identify Explain what causes STIs and how they are transmitted.

6 Explain How does a fetus get nourishment up until the time it is born?

The fetus gets oxygen and nourishment from an organ called the placenta.

Use the graph to answer the following question.

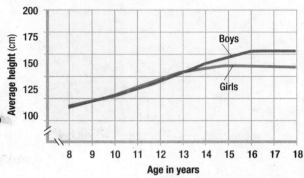

Growth Rates in Boys and Girls

Source: Centers for Disease Control and Prevention

7 Interpret At what age is the difference between the average height of boys and girls greatest? Estimate this difference to the nearest centimeter.

Critical Thinking

8 Predict How might cancer of the testes affect a man's ability to make sperm?

9 Apply Explain the difference beween identical twins and fraternal twins. Include in your answer how they form and their genetic makeup.

Identical twins form when one sperm fertilizes one egg, then the developing embr

My Notes

Unit 1 Big Idea

The human body is made up of systems that have different functions, and these systems work together to maintain the body.

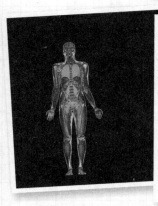

Lesson 1
ESSENTIAL QUESTION
How do the body systems work together to maintain homeostasis?

Describe the functions of the human body systems, including how they work together to maintain homeostasis.

Lesson 2
ESSENTIAL QUESTION
How do your skeletal and muscular systems work?

Explain how the skeletal and muscular systems work together to allow movement of the body.

Lesson 3
ESSENTIAL QUESTION
How do the circulatory and respiratory systems work?

Relate the structures of the circulatory and respiratory systems to their functions in the human body.

Lesson 4
ESSENTIAL QUESTION
How do your body's digestive and excretory systems work?

Relate the parts of the digestive and excretory systems to their roles in the human body.

Lesson 5
ESSENTIAL QUESTION
How do the nervous and endocrine systems work?

Relate the structures of the nervous and endocrine systems to their functions in the human body.

Lesson 6
ESSENTIAL QUESTION
How does your reproductive system work?

Relate the structure of the reproductive system to its function in the human body.

Connect ESSENTIAL QUESTIONS
Lessons 5 and 6

1 Explain How does the endocrine system regulate the function of the reproductive system in males and females?

_____

_____

_____

_____

Think Outside the Book

2 Synthesize Choose one of these activities to help synthesize what you have learned in this unit.

☐ Using what you learned in lessons 1 through 6, choose a human body system and create a poster presentation to explain its structures and functions.

☐ Using what you learned in lessons 2, 3, 4, and 5, write a short story that explains which body systems are involved when a person eats an apple.

Name _____

Vocabulary

Fill in each blank with the term that best completes the following sentences.

1 _____ is the maintenance of a stable environment inside the body.

2 The _____ are the specialized tubes in the kidneys in which waste is collected from the blood.

3 A place where two or more bones are connected is called a(n) _____.

4 The _____ is the body system that controls growth, metabolism, and regulates reproduction through hormones.

5 The _____ is the female reproductive organ that produces egg cells.

Key Concepts

Read each question below, and circle the best answer.

6 Which of these statements correctly describes a key difference between aerobic activity and anaerobic activity?

A Aerobic activity is intense and of short duration, while anaerobic activity involves moderate effort over a long period of time.

B Muscles do not use oxygen during aerobic activity, but they do during anaerobic activity.

C Aerobic activity increases muscle endurance, while anaerobic activity increases muscle strength.

D Lifting weights is an aerobic activity, while jogging is an anaerobic activity.

7 Which of these body systems is made up of the tissues and organs responsible for collecting fluid that leaks from the blood and returning it to the blood?

A excretory system   **C** endocrine system

B cardiovascular system   **D** lymphatic system

8 The diagram below shows the main parts of the respiratory system.

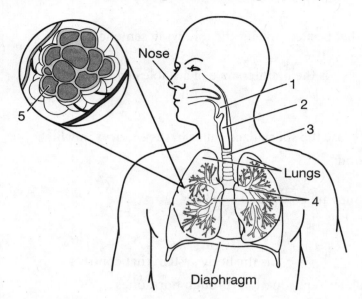

Which of these correctly names the parts of the respiratory system numbered 1 through 5 in the diagram above?

A 1. larynx, 2. pharynx, 3. trachea, 4. bronchi, 5. alveoli

B 1. pharynx, 2. larynx, 3. trachea, 4. bronchi, 5. alveoli

C 1. pharynx, 2. larynx, 3. bronchi, 4. trachea, 5. alveoli

D 1. larynx, 2. trachea, 3. pharynx, 4. alveoli, 5. bronchi

9 Which of these correctly maps the circulation of blood from the heart through the blood vessels and back to the heart?

A heart → arteries → capillaries → veins → heart

B heart → veins→ capillaries → arteries → heart

C heart → capillaries → arteries → veins → capillaries → heart

D heart → arteries → capillaries → veins → capillaries → heart

10 Which of the following sentences best describes the esophagus?

A It produces bile that helps the digestive system break down fats.

B It is a muscular tube that moves food from the mouth to the stomach.

C It releases enzymes into the small intestine that aid in chemical digestion.

D It is a muscular bag that churns food and produces acid and enzymes for chemical digestion.

11 The diagram below shows two important parts of the human digestive system.

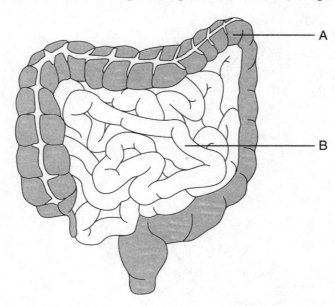

Which of these statements is correct?

A Part A absorbs most of the nutrients from digested food into the bloodstream.

B The pancreas releases enzymes into part A to aid in chemical digestion.

C As food digests, it moves through part B first, then through part A.

D The inside of part A is covered with finger-like projections called villi.

12 Which of the following is a correct statement about the role of the kidney in homeostasis?

A The kidney helps to keep smooth muscle contracting efficiently.

B The kidney filters wastes, such as sodium, from the blood.

C The kidney stores bile, which breaks down fats in the intestine.

D The kidney works with the endocrine system to help the body react to stimuli that occur outside the body.

13 Which of these glands of the endocrine system would you suspect has a problem if someone has an abnormal level of sugar in the blood?

A pineal gland

C pancreas

B parathyroid

D pituitary gland

14 Which of these pictures shows a nerve cell?

A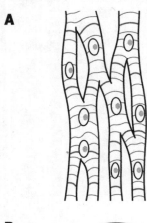

C

B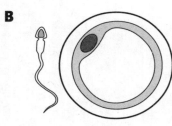

D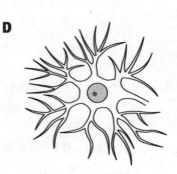

15 Which development occurs in the second trimester of pregnancy?

A The eyes of the fetus first open and blink.

B The embryo becomes a fetus.

C The embryo moves from the fallopian tube to the uterus.

D Contractions in the uterus move the fetus from the uterus through the vaginal canal.

16 Which of these is a function of the testes?

A to produce egg cells

B to produce a hormone that causes facial hair to grow

C to produce a hormone that causes growth of wider hips

D to deliver semen into the female reproductive system

Critical Thinking

Answer the following questions in the space provided.

17 The diagram below shows some of the muscles and bones of the arm.

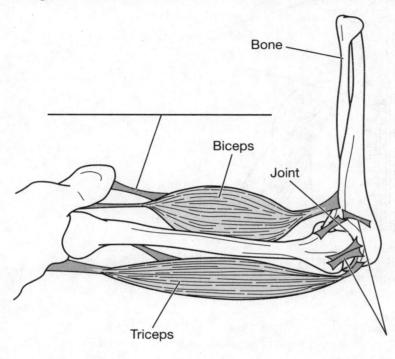

Fill in the blank lines in the diagram above to label the two types of connective tissue shown, then describe the function of each below.

_____

_____

_____

18 Explain the difference between pulmonary circulation and systemic circulation.

_____

_____

_____

_____

_____

_____

_____

19 The diagram below shows the two main parts of the human nervous system.

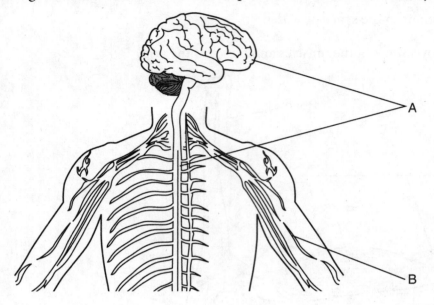

Write the names for the two parts of the nervous system labeled A and B.
Then describe the main functions of each part.

A Name: _____

Function: _____

B Name: _____

Function: _____

Connect **ESSENTIAL QUESTIONS**
Lessons 1, 2, 3, and 5

Answer the following question in the space provided.

20 When you burn yourself after touching something hot, you pull your hand away
quickly. Use what you learned in lessons 1, 2, 3, and 5 to describe how your
skeletal, muscular, circulatory, endocrine, and nervous systems work together to
make you react and to start healing your burn.

_____

_____

_____

_____

_____

_____

_____

Human Health

© Houghton Mifflin Harcourt Publishing Company • Image Credits: (bkgd) ©Steve Gschmeissner/Photo Researchers, Inc.; (br) ©Myrleen Pearson/Alamy

Big Idea

A healthy immune system, good nutrition, and physical activity are all important in the maintenance of the human body.

Tapeworms attach themselves to the intestinal wall with these hooks.

What do you think?

Tapeworms can be passed between infected animals and people. Tapeworms make organisms sick by absorbing nutrients more quickly than their host can. How does your body respond to infectious disease?

Keeping your pets healthy can help keep you healthy.

CITIZEN SCIENCE

Stop the Flu!

Many diseases spread through contact between infected people. Simple measures can help stop diseases from spreading.

① Think About It

A Take a quick survey of the students in your class to find out how many have had the flu in the past year. Record your findings here.

_____
_____
_____

B Ask students who have had the flu to describe the symptoms they had. Record the symptoms below.

_____
_____
_____

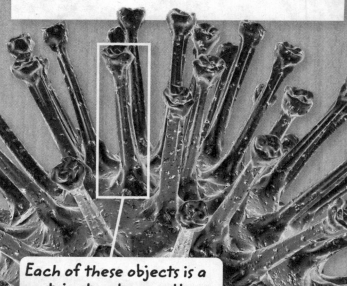

Each of these objects is a protein structure on the surface of a single flu virus.

© Houghton Mifflin Harcourt Publishing Company • Image Credits: (br) ©Pasieka/Photo Researchers, Inc.; (tr) ©Pasieka/Photo Researchers, Inc.

② Ask A Question

How do you fight a flu?

The flu is caused by a family of viruses. Viruses are tiny particles that attach to the surface of the cells in the body. But how do they get there? With your class, conduct research to answer the questions below:

A How is the flu spread?

_____

_____

B What are common ways to prevent the spread of the flu?

_____

_____

_____

Wash your hands.

Sneeze into your sleeve.

Use a tissue.

③ Make A Plan

A Choose one or two of the ways to fight the flu that you would like your whole school to do.

_____

_____

B In the space below, sketch out a design for a poster or pamphlet that would inform students of how they can avoid the flu.

C Once you have created your pamphlets or posters, write down how you plan to give out the pamphlets or where you would place the posters.

_____

_____

_____

_____

_____

_____

_____

_____

_____

_____

Take It Home

Take your pamphlet or poster home. Use the pamphlet or poster to explain to everyone at home how they, too, can avoid the flu.

The Immune System

Parasitic worm

ESSENTIAL QUESTION

How does your body's defense system work?

By the end of this lesson, you should be able to explain how the immune system fights infection.

Macrophage

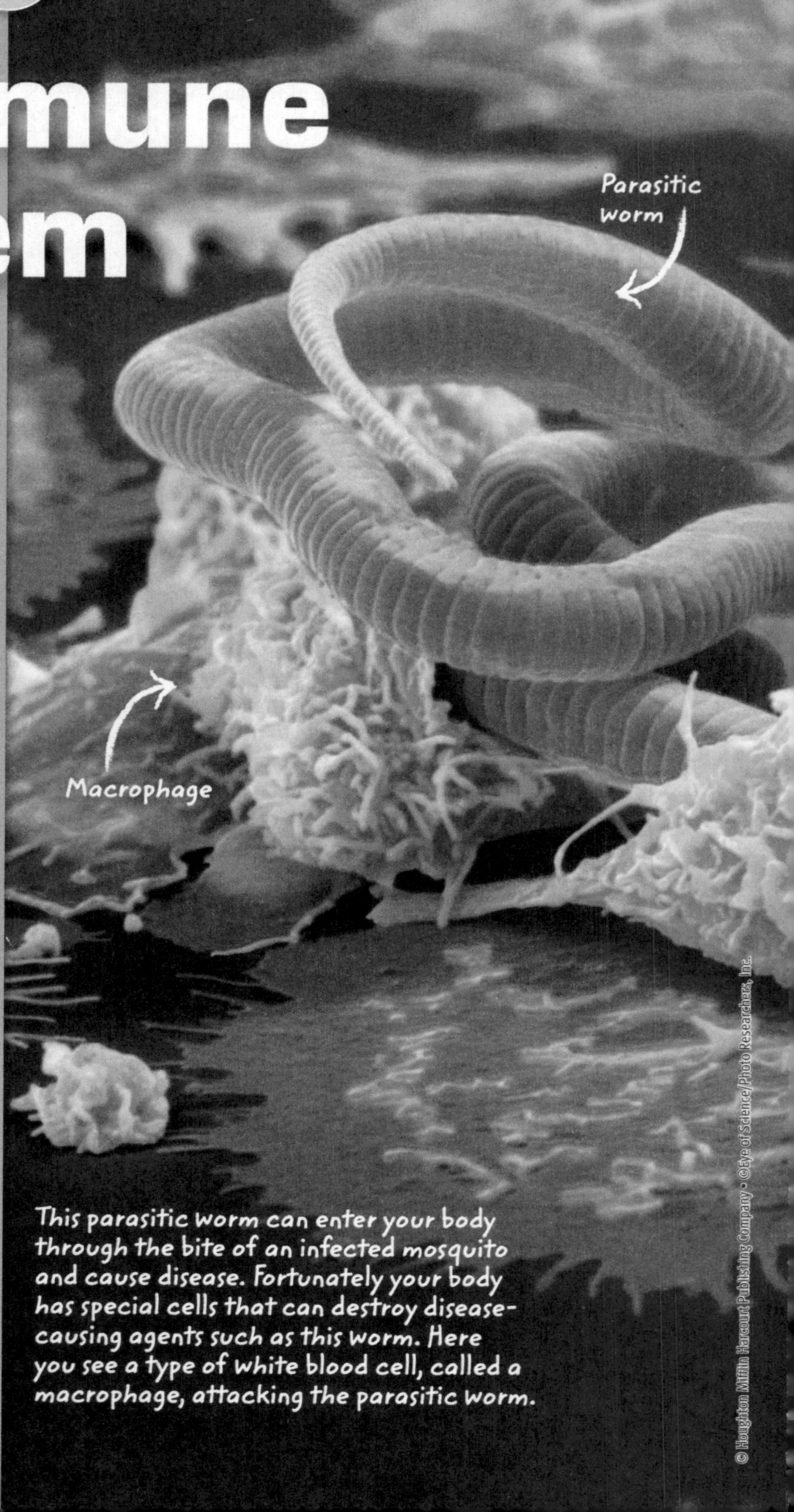

This parasitic worm can enter your body through the bite of an infected mosquito and cause disease. Fortunately your body has special cells that can destroy disease-causing agents such as this worm. Here you see a type of white blood cell, called a macrophage, attacking the parasitic worm.

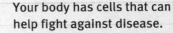

Lesson Labs

Quick Labs
- How Does Skin Provide Protection?
- Memory Cells
- Mucus Lining

Exploration Lab
- Modeling the Immune Response

Engage Your Brain

1 Infer What happens when a computer gets a virus?

_____

_____

_____

_____

_____

2 Predict Check T or F to show whether you think each statement is true or false.

T	F	
	☐	Your body has cells that can help fight against disease.
☐	☐	Most microscopic organisms are harmless.
☐	☐	Skin can protect against infection.
☐	☐	Fever is always harmful to the body.

Active Reading

3 Synthesize You can often define an unknown word if you know the meaning of its word parts. Use the word parts and sentence below to make an educated guess about the meaning of the word *pathogen*.

Word part	Meaning
patho-	disease
-gen	to bring forth

Example sentence
Your body is constantly protecting itself against pathogens.

pathogen:

_____

_____

Vocabulary Terms

- pathogen
- immune system
- macrophage
- T cell
- B cell
- antibody
- immunity
- vaccine

4 Apply As you learn the definition of each vocabulary term in this lesson, create your own definition or sketch to help you remember the meaning of the term.

Playing DEFENSE

Inquiry

5 Describe How might watery eyes be a defensive response?

Watery eyes flush out pathogens

What is your body's defense system?

Microscopic organisms and particles, such as bacteria and viruses, are all around you. Most are harmless, but some can make you sick. A **pathogen** is an organism, a virus, or a protein that causes disease. Fortunately, your body has many ways to protect you from pathogens.

External Defenses

Your skin provides external protection against pathogens that may enter the body. Skin also has structures, such as hair, nails, and sweat and oil glands, that help provide protection. For example, glands in your skin secrete oil that can kill pathogens. Mucus produced by mucous membranes in your nose and saliva in your mouth wash pathogens down into your stomach, where most are quickly digested. Hair, such as eyelashes and ear hairs, keep many particles in the air from entering the body. Nails protect your fingertips and toes. The skin and all of these structures make up the _integumentary system_.

External Defense Example

Your body loses and replaces approximately 1 million skin cells every 40 min. In the process, countless pathogens are removed.

6 Apply Why is it important to clean and care for cuts on your skin?

So pathogens don't get in

Internal Defenses

Most of the time, pathogens cannot get past external defenses. Sometimes, skin is cut and pathogens can enter the body. The body responds quickly to keep out as many pathogens as possible. Blood flow increases to the injured area, causing it to swell and turn red. This swelling and redness is called *inflammation*. Cell pieces in the blood, called *platelets*, help seal the open wound so that no more pathogens can enter.

Your body may also respond by raising your body temperature. This response is called *fever*, which slows the growth of bacteria and some other pathogens. Both inflammation and fever are a part of the body's internal defenses. If a pathogen is not destroyed by inflammation or fever, then the immune system responds.

The **immune system** is made up of tissues and specialized white blood cells that recognize and attack foreign substances in the body. These white blood cells function in a coordinated way to identify and destroy pathogens.

7 Recognize List some of the body's external and internal defenses.

External Defenses
hair
nails
sneezing
coughing

Internal Defenses
fever
inflammation

Do the Math

We usually measure temperature in degrees Fahrenheit (°F), but the standard scientific scale is in degrees Celsius (°C).

Sample Problems

To convert from °F to °C, first subtract 32 from the °F temperature, then multiply by 5, then divide by 9.

Normal body temperature is 98.6 °F. What is this temperature in °C?

$$(98.6\ °F - 32) \times 5 \div 9 = 37\ °C$$

To convert from °C to °F, first multiply the °C temperature by 9, then divide by 5, then add 32.

$$(37\ °C \times 9) \div 5 + 32 = 98.6\ °F$$

You Try It

8 Calculate If you have a fever, and your temperature is 39 °C, what is your temperature in °F?

102.2 °F

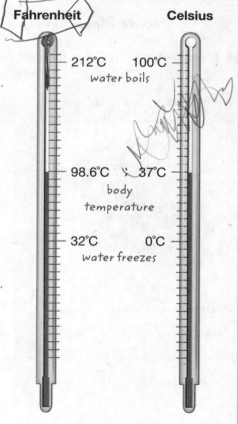

Fahrenheit — Celsius

212°C   100°C
water boils

98.6°C   37°C
body temperature

32°C   0°C
water freezes

Search and DESTROY

Active Reading

9 Identify As you read, underline the characteristics of an antigen.

A macrophage is a white blood cell that attacks pathogens.

What are some white blood cells that protect the body?

White blood cells destroy invading pathogens. Unlike red blood cells, white blood cells can move out of the blood vessels and "patrol" all the tissues of the body. Some of these cells attack pathogens directly. A **macrophage** (MAK•ruh•faj) is a white blood cell that destroys pathogens by engulfing and digesting them. Macrophages help start the body's immune response to *antigens*. An antigen is a substance that stimulates a response by the immune system. An antigen can be a pathogen or any foreign material in the body.

The immune system consists mainly of *T cells* and *B cells*. Some **T cells** coordinate the body's immune response, while others attack infected cells. T cells known as *helper T cells* activate other T cells, called *killer T cells*. Killer T cells attack infected body cells by attaching to specific antigens. Helper T cells also activate B cells. Once activated, **B cells** make antibodies that attach to specific antigens. An **antibody** is a specialized protein that binds to a specific antigen to tag it for destruction.

White Blood Cells

10 Identify Write in the main function, or task, of each white blood cell.

Macrophage	T cell	B cell
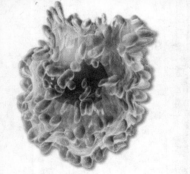	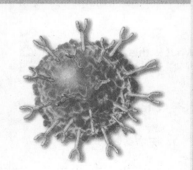	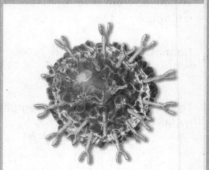
Nickname: Destroyer	Nickname: Activator/Attacker	Nickname: Responder
Task: Englufs and digests pathogens	Task: Attack infected body cells.	Task: Make antibodies

Visualize It!

The Immune Response

11 Diagram Trace the path of the B cell response using a solid line. Trace the path of the T cell response using a dashed line.

A virus that enters the body may be destroyed by macrophages, or the virus may get through to infect a body cell.

Virus

Viral antigen

Virus

Macrophages engulf the virus particles and show the viral antigen. These macrophages activate helper T cells.

Macrophage

Receptor protein

Helper T cell

Helper T cell

Helper T cells recognize the viral antigen on the macrophages. Helper T cells trigger two responses: the T cell response and the B cell response.

Helper T cell

B cell response

Helper T cells activate B cells to make and release antibodies that recognize the shape of the viral antigen.

T cell response

Helper T cells activate killer T cells.

B cell

Killer T cell

Activated B cell

Antibody

Viral antigen

Antibodies bind to the viral antigens, forming clumps, and tag the virus for destruction. An antibody's shape is specialized to match an antigen like a key fits a lock.

Infected body cell

Killer T cells recognize the viral antigen on infected body cells. The killer T cells destroy the infected cells and cause the cells to release the virus particles.

Virus

12 Compare How do helper T cells differ from B cells?

B cells make antibodies. Helper T cells detect pathogens.

© Houghton Mifflin Harcourt Publishing Company

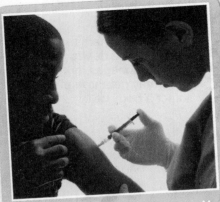

Vaccinations build immunity. This young person is receiving a vaccination shot.

Shields UP!

How does the body build immunity?

The body builds immunity against a disease when it is exposed to the pathogen that causes the disease. **Immunity** is the ability to resist or recover from an infectious disease. Immunity is passed from a mother to her fetus. Immunity can also result from the body being infected with the disease or from the body being vaccinated.

Producing Memory Cells

Your body produces billions of different kinds of T cells and B cells. However, it doesn't produce very many of each kind for specific pathogens. But, once your body has fought a pathogen, the body produces *memory cells*. Memory cells are T cells and B cells that "remember" a specific pathogen. Memory cells are not activated until the pathogen enters your body. Once the pathogen enters, your body immediately starts making large numbers of T cells and B cells that attack the pathogen. Your memory cells have made you immune to the pathogen.

Vaccination

A **vaccine** is a substance prepared from killed or weakened pathogens that is introduced into the body to produce immunity. The vaccine stimulates the body to make an immune response. B cells make antibodies to attack the specific pathogen being injected. Vaccination, or immunization, is a way to prevent illness from some diseases. Vaccines are used to trigger the body to make memory cells for a specific pathogen without causing illness.

Think Outside the Book

13 Apply Think about the different ways that we record memories, such as writing in a journal or taking photographs. Journals, photographs, odors, and many other things can trigger details about a memory. Describe at least one way in which you record your memories.

How a Vaccine Works

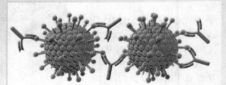

The vaccine is prepared from a killed or weakened pathogen and is introduced into the body.

The immune system responds, producing T cells and activated B cells. Memory cells are also produced.

If the pathogen infects the body, T cells and B cells begin a new immune response against the pathogen.

14 Synthesize How are vaccines related to memory cells?

Memory cells remember how to attack the vaccine so when the body gets the real disease, it can fight it

What can challenge the immune system?

The immune system is a very effective body defense system. However, sometimes the immune system doesn't work properly and disease results. This can occur when a person inherits a gene that prevents the immune system from developing properly. It can also happen as a result of some kinds of infection.

Challenges to the Immune System

Allergies	Sometimes, a person's immune system reacts to foreign antigens that are not dangerous to most people. An immune system reaction to a harmless or common substance is called an *allergy*. Allergies can be caused by certain foods such as peanuts, medicines such as penicillin, or certain types of pollen and molds.	**15 Relate** List different allergies that you or someone you know may have. Pollen, Cats, peanuts
Cancer	Healthy cells divide at a carefully controlled rate. Sometimes, cells don't respond to the body's controls. *Cancer* is a group of diseases in which cells divide at an uncontrolled rate. The immune system may not be able to stop the cancer cells from growing. Skin cancer is often caused by exposure to ultraviolet rays from sunlight, which can affect the cells that make pigment.	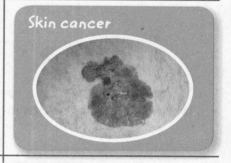 Skin cancer
Immune Deficiency	The immune system sometimes fails to develop properly or becomes weakened, resulting in an *immune deficiency disorder*. Acquired immune deficiency syndrome (AIDS) is caused by human immunodeficiency virus (HIV). This virus specifically infects the helper T cells. When the number of helper T cells becomes very low, neither T cell nor B cell immune responses can be activated. People who have AIDS can become very ill from pathogens that a healthy body can easily control.	**16 Relate** What is the relationship between HIV and AIDS? AIDS is caused by HIV. People with AIDS can become very ill from pathogens that a healthy body can easily control.
Auto-immune Diseases	A disease in which the immune system attacks the body's own cells is called an *autoimmune disease*. In an autoimmune disease, immune system cells mistake body cells for foreign antigens. For example, rheumatoid arthritis (ROO•muh•toid ahr•THRY•tis) is a disease in which the immune system attacks the joints, most commonly the joints of the hands, as shown here.	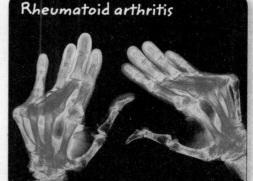 Rheumatoid arthritis

Visual Summary

To complete this summary, circle the correct word. Then use the key below to check your answers. You can use this page to review the main concepts of the lesson.

The Immune System

The human body has external and internal defenses.

17 This type of defense is external / internal.

18 This type of defense is external / internal.

39 °C

The immune system has a specialized internal immune response when pathogens invade the body.

19 This is a macrophage/B cell engulfing a pathogen.

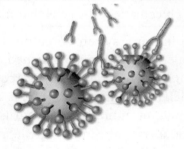

20 This is a(n) antibody / macrophage attaching to an antigen.

Answers: 17 external; 18 internal; 19 macrophage; 20 antibody

21 Summarize Explain three ways that your body can defend itself against pathogens.

Lesson Review

Vocabulary

In your own words, define the following terms.

1 pathogen

_____

_____

_____

2 immune system

_____

_____

_____

Key Concepts

3 List What are some of your body's external defenses against pathogens?

_____

_____

_____

4 Summarize Explain how an immune response starts after a macrophage attacks a pathogen.

_____

_____

_____

_____

_____

_____

_____

5 Compare How do T cells differ from B cells?

_____

_____

_____

_____

Critical Thinking

Use the graph to answer the following question.

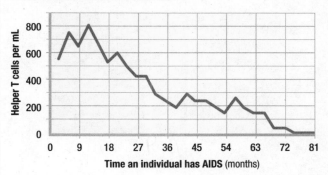

T Cell Count of a Person with AIDS

6 Interpret Over time, people with AIDS become very sick and are unable to fight off infection. Use the information in the graph to explain why this occurs.

_____

_____

_____

_____

7 Explain How does your body respond differently the second time it is exposed to a pathogen than the first time it was exposed to the same pathogen?

_____

_____

_____

_____

8 Infer Can your body make antibodies for pathogens that you have never been in contact with? Why or why not?

_____

_____

_____

_____

My Notes

Mean, Median, Mode, and Range

You will often find that the samples you study in science vary in size. How do you estimate the size of such varying data sets? You can analyze both the measures of central tendency and the variability of data using mean, median, mode, and range.

Tutorial

Imagine that a public health research group is comparing the number of cases of flu in a specific country. Data has been collected for the last five years.

When working with numerical data, it is helpful to find a value that describes the data set. These representative values can describe a typical data value, or describe how spread out the data values are.

Number of Cases of Flu	
Year	**Number of Cases**
2004	800
2005	300
2006	150
2007	300
2008	200

Mean The mean is the sum of all of the values in a data set divided by the total number of values in the data set. The mean is also called the *average*.	$$\frac{800 + 300 + 150 + 300 + 200}{5}$$ **mean** = 350 cases/year
Median The median is the value of the middle item when data are arranged in numerical order. If there is an odd number of values, the median is the middle value. If there is an even number of values, the median is the mean of the two middle values.	If necessary, reorder the values from least to greatest: 150, 200, 300, 300, 800 ⟶ ⟵ 300 is the middle value **median** = 300 cases/year
Mode The mode is the value or values that occur most frequently in a data set. If all values occur with the same frequency, the data set is said to have no mode. Values should be put in order to find the mode.	If necessary, reorder the values from least to greatest: 150, 200, 300, 300, 800 The value 300 occurs most frequently. **mode** = 300 cases/year
Range Range is another way to measure data. It measures how variable, or spread out, the data are. The range is the difference between the greatest value and the least value of a data set.	$$800 - 150 = 650$$ **range** = 650

You Try It!

The data table below shows the reported number of flu cases in four different countries.

Reported Number of Cases of Flu				
Year	Country 1	Country 2	Country 3	Country 4
2004	800	none	650	750
2005	300	350	450	450
2006	150	450	500	400
2007	300	200	550	350
2008	200	350	600	600

①

Using Formulas Find the mean, median, and mode of the data for Country 2.

②

Using Formulas Find the mean, median, and mode of the data for Country 3.

③

Analyzing Data Find the mean number of reported flu cases for only years in which cases were reported in Country 2. Compare this with the mean value for all years in Country 2. What conclusion can you draw about the effect of zeros on the mean of a data set?

Mean number of cases for years in which cases were reported: _____

Mean number of cases for all years: _____

Effect of zeros on the mean:

_____

_____

④

Evaluating Data Would the country with the greatest total number of flu cases from 2004 to 2008 have the greatest mean? Explain your reasoning.

_____

_____

_____

⑤

Analyzing Methods Calculate the range for Country 3.

When do you think you might need to use range instead of mean, median or mode?

_____

_____

_____

Infectious Disease

ESSENTIAL QUESTION

What causes disease?

By the end of this lesson, you should be able to compare types of infectious agents that may infect the human body.

This may look like a spaceship landing and taking off of a planet. In fact, this is a virus injecting its DNA into a bacterial cell. The bacteria will copy the viral DNA, making more viruses.

Lesson Labs

Quick Labs
• Passing the Cold
• Spreading a Disease
Exploration Lab
• Killing Bacteria

Engage Your Brain

1 Predict Check T or F to show whether you think each statement is true or false.

T	F	
☐	☐	Diseases cannot be treated.
☐	☐	Handwashing can help prevent the spread of disease.
☐	☐	Only bacteria and viruses cause disease.
☐	☐	All diseases can be spread from one person to another.

2 Explain Explain what you think the term *infection* means.

_____
_____
_____
_____
_____
_____
_____
_____

Active Reading

3 Synthesize You can often define an unknown word if you know the meaning of its word parts. Use the word parts and sentence below to make an educated guess about the meaning of the word *antibiotic*.

Word part	Meaning
anti-	against
bio-	life

Example sentence
Antibiotics are used to treat bacterial illnesses such as strep throat.

Vocabulary Terms
• noninfectious disease
• infectious disease
• antibiotic
• antiviral drug

4 Identify This list contains the key terms you'll learn in this lesson. As you read, circle the definition of each term.

antibiotic:

_____
_____

What is a noninfectious disease?

When you have a disease, your body does not function normally. You may feel tired, or have a sore throat, or have pain in your joints. Diseases have specific *symptoms,* or changes in how a person feels because of an illness. While there are many different kinds of diseases, all diseases can be categorized as either *noninfectious disease* or *infectious disease.*

Diseases that are caused by hereditary or environmental factors are called **noninfectious diseases**. For example, type I diabetes is caused by hereditary factors. Type 1 diabetes destroys cells that produce insulin. This makes it difficult for the body to use sugar for energy. Hemophilia is also caused by hereditary factors. The blood of people who have hemophilia does not clot properly when they get a cut. Some noninfectious diseases can be caused by environmental factors. *Mutagens* are environmental factors that cause mutations, or changes, in DNA. Sometimes, the changes cause a cell to reproduce uncontrollably. This results in a disease called *cancer.* X-rays, cigarette smoke, some air pollutants, and UV rays in sunlight can cause cancer. Cancer can have both hereditary and environmental causes.

Active Reading

5 List Name two types of factors that cause noninfectious disease.

_____

_____

_____

People who work around radiation, such as x-ray technicians, must protect themselves from overexposure.

X-RAYS CONTROLLED AREA

No unauthorised entry

Think Outside the Book Inquiry

6 Relate Think about a job that requires protection against some type of contamination. Then do the following:

- Explain why protection is necessary for that job.
- Draw the method of protection used for that job.

Air pollution can cause respiratory disease.

What is an infectious disease?

A disease that is caused by a *pathogen* is called an **infectious disease**. Pathogens include bacteria, fungi, and parasites, which are all alive. Pathogens also include viruses, which are noncellular particles that depend on living things to reproduce. Viruses cannot function on their own, so they are not considered to be alive.

Pathogens that cause disease can be picked up from the environment or passed from one living thing to another. Some pathogens travel through the air. Sneezing and coughing can release thousands of tiny droplets that may carry pathogens. If a person inhales these droplets, he or she may become infected. Some pathogens can be passed from nonliving things. A rusty nail can carry tetanus bacteria that may cause disease if a person is scratched by the nail. Pathogens can also be passed by other living things. Many diseases are carried by fleas, ticks, and mosquitoes.

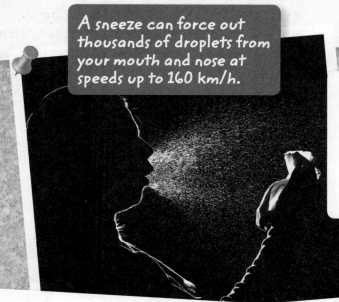

A sneeze can force out thousands of droplets from your mouth and nose at speeds up to 160 km/h.

7 Apply What can you do to reduce the spread of droplets when you sneeze or cough?

_____

_____

_____

8 Categorize Determine whether each disease is infectious or noninfectious, and put a check mark in the correct box.

Example	Noninfectious Disease	Infectious Disease
Emphysema caused by cigarette smoke		
Strep throat that's been going around school		
Skin cancer caused by too much sun exposure		
The flu that you and your family members have		

That's Sick!

What can cause infectious disease?

Each type of pathogen causes a specific infectious disease. But diseases caused by similar types of pathogens share some common characteristics. Knowing what type of pathogen causes a disease helps doctors know how to treat the disease.

Viruses

Viruses are tiny particles that have their own genetic material but depend on living things to reproduce. Viruses insert their genetic material into a cell, and then the cell makes more viruses. Many viruses cause disease. Some, such as cold and flu viruses, are spread through the air or by contact. Others, such as the human immunodeficiency virus, or HIV, are spread through the transfer of body fluids. There are many types of cold and flu viruses, so preventing a cold or flu can be difficult.

👁 **Visualize It!**

9 Apply Once inside, what part of the cell do the viral particles go to? What do they do there?

_____

_____

_____

Bacteria

Most bacteria are beneficial to other living things. However, some bacteria cause disease. For example, the bacterium that causes tuberculosis infects about one-third of the world's population. It can infect a variety of organs, including the lungs, where it slowly destroys lung tissue. Strep throat, diarrheal illness, and some types of sinus infections are also caused by bacteria.

10 List Name some diseases caused by bacteria.

_____

_____

_____

_____

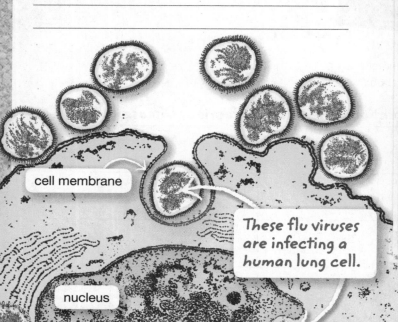

cell membrane

nucleus

These flu viruses are infecting a human lung cell.

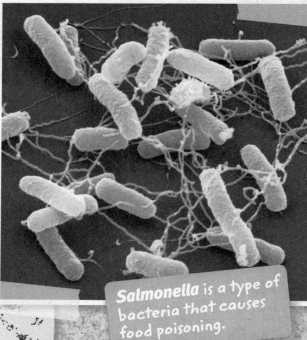

Salmonella is a type of bacteria that causes food poisoning.

Fungi

Most fungi are beneficial because they decompose, or break down, dead plants and animals into materials that other organisms use. However, some fungi are pathogens. The most common fungal diseases are skin infections. Two of the most common fungal skin infections are athlete's foot and ringworm of the body and scalp. These fungal skin infections can be passed on through contact with an infected person or contact with items such as socks, shoes, and shower surfaces where the fungus can grow.

11 Explain Why are most fungi beneficial?

_____

_____

_____

Parasites

A *parasite* is an organism that lives on and feeds on another organism, called a *host*. Parasites usually harm the host. Some of the most common parasites in humans are certain types of single-celled organisms called *protists*. For example, the protists that cause malaria infect as many as 500 million people each year. Another disease, called giardiasis, occurs when people consume water or food contaminated with the protist *Giardia lamblia*. Worms can also be parasites. The roundworm *Ascaris lumbricoides* is the most common cause of parasitic worm infections. It is spread in contaminated food, such as unwashed fruits and vegetables.

Active Reading **12 Define** What is a parasite?

_____

_____

_____

ringworm infection

Despite its name, ringworm is caused by a fungus, not by a worm.

Giardia lamblia is a protist parasite that can cause stomach cramps, nausea, and diarrhea. Filtering water can help prevent infections from this protist.

Giardia lamblia

Don't Pass It On

How can infectious diseases be transmitted?

Some scientists who investigate infectious diseases focus on the ways that diseases are passed on, or transmitted. A disease that spreads from person to person is a *contagious* disease. A person is also considered to be contagious if he or she has a disease that can spread to other people. Diseases can also be transmitted to people by other organisms and by contaminated food, water, or objects.

Water and Food

Drinking water in the United States is generally safe. But if a water treatment system fails, the water could become contaminated. Untreated water, such as rivers and streams, can also carry pathogens. Bacteria in foods can cause illness, too. For example, cattle and chickens often carry *Salmonella* bacteria. Raw beef, chicken, and eggs should be handled carefully during preparation to avoid contaminating food.

13 Infer Why should raw meats be kept separate from other foods?

_____

_____

Person to Person

Many diseases that affect the respiratory system are passed from one person to another through the air by a sneeze or cough. The common cold, the flu, and tuberculosis are usually spread this way. Pathogens can also be passed when an infected person touches another person. Other diseases, such as acquired immune deficiency syndrome, or AIDS, and hepatitis C can be passed during sexual contact.

14 Recognize List three ways that disease can be transmitted from one person to another.

_____

_____

_____

Deer tick that can transmit Lyme disease

Animals to People

Quite a few human diseases are transmitted to humans by animals, especially insects and ticks. For example, humans can become infected with malaria when they are bitten by a mosquito infected with the malaria parasite. In a similar way, certain species of ticks can transmit diseases such as Rocky Mountain spotted fever and Lyme disease. Animals infected with the rabies virus can pass the disease on to other animals or people through a bite that cuts the skin.

Contaminated Objects

Objects that are handled by sick people or that come in contact with infected animals or contaminated food can pick up pathogens. Drinking glasses, utensils, doorknobs, towels, keyboards, and many other objects can transfer pathogens from one person to another. People who inject illegal drugs, such as heroin, can easily pick up pathogens from contaminated needles and related items. Traces of contaminated blood on a needle can infect a person who shares that needle.

15 Predict Read the scenario in the table below, and explain how disease could be transmitted to other people.

Scenario	How could disease be transmitted?
A person with a cold sneezes in a bus full of people.	
A person with a skin fungus shares a towel with another person.	

End Transmission

refrigeration

pasteurization

pickling

A variety of technologies used today allow some foods to be stored longer.

How can diseases be reduced?

Several important changes have helped decrease the occurrence of infectious disease. These changes include improved personal hygiene and improved technology used in medical procedures and food preservation.

Today, vaccines are used all over the world to prevent many serious diseases. Modern medical procedures using sterilized equipment, gloves, and masks help reduce contamination and improve patient recovery. Modern canning, freezing, dehydration, pickling, and refrigeration help prevent contamination of food. Pasteurization (pas•cher•ih•ZAY•shuhn) is the controlled heating of beverages or food, such as milk and cheese, to kill bacteria.

16 Apply Which methods of food preservation do you use at home?

_____

_____

_____

How can disease be treated?

Scientists are constantly discovering new ways to fight disease. *Antibiotics* have had a major impact on fighting some pathogens. An **antibiotic** is a medicine used to kill or slow the growth of bacteria and other microorganisms, such as fungi. Viruses, such as those that cause colds, are not affected by antibiotics. An antibiotic blocks cell processes. A virus relies on its host cell to survive, and does not have its own cell processes for the antibiotic to block. Today, *antiviral drugs* are being developed and used to treat viral infections. An **antiviral drug** is a drug that destroys viruses or prevents their replication.

Active Reading

17 Identify As you read, underline the types of pathogens that are affected by antibiotics.

Resisting ARREST

A microscopic world of organisms exists all around us. Bacteria live in your mouth, on your skin, and on many objects that you touch every day. Most bacteria are harmless. However, some strains of bacteria that cause disease are no longer affected by antibiotics.

Tough guys
Some strains of *Staphylococcus aureus* bacteria have developed a resistance to antibiotics.

The Value of Money
Your money may carry more than just value. At least 93 different types of bacteria have been identified on dollar bills. Think of all the places each bill has traveled!

Soap It Up
Being in contact with different people and objects increases your exposure to a variety of microscopic organisms. Washing your hands throughout the day can help reduce your risk for some infections.

Extend

Inquiry

18 Identify What is the name and type of pathogen discussed in this article?

19 Research *Salmonella* is a pathogen that can be transmitted by contaminated food. Research and describe how *Salmonella* could be transmitted from a food processing factory to you.

20 Apply Find an object in your school that you and your classmates come in contact with nearly every day. How can you protect yourself and others from pathogens that may be on the object?

Visual Summary

To complete this summary, fill in the blanks with the correct word or phrase. Then, use the key below to check your answers. You can use this page to review the main concepts of the lesson.

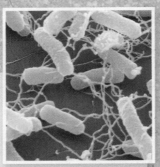

Diseases are categorized as noninfectious disease or infectious disease.

21 A disease that can be passed from one person to another is a(n)

_____

Infectious disease can be caused by different types of pathogens.

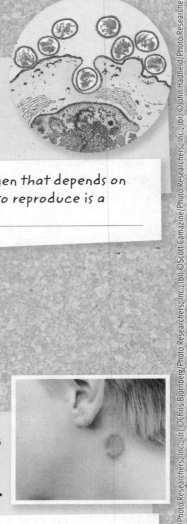

22 A type of pathogen that depends on living organisms to reproduce is a

_____

Infectious Disease

Infectious disease can be transmitted in many different ways.

23 List four ways an infectious disease can be transmitted.

_____

_____

_____

_____

The spread of infectious diseases can be reduced, and some diseases can be treated.

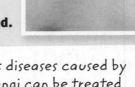

24 Some infectious diseases caused by bacteria and fungi can be treated using

_____

Answers: 21 Infectious disease; 22 virus; 23 another person, some animals, water and food, contaminated objects; 24 antibiotics

25 Synthesis Explain why antibiotics cannot be used to treat noninfectious disease.

_____

Lesson Review

Vocabulary

In your own words, define the following terms.

1 noninfectious disease

_____

_____

_____

2 infectious disease

_____

_____

_____

Key Concepts

3 Identify Name four types of pathogens that could cause infectious disease.

_____

_____

_____

_____

4 Justify How has technology helped to reduce the spread of infectious disease?

_____

_____

_____

_____

_____

_____

_____

5 Compare How do viruses differ from bacteria, fungi, and parasites?

_____

_____

_____

_____

_____

Critical Thinking

Use the graph to answer the following questions.

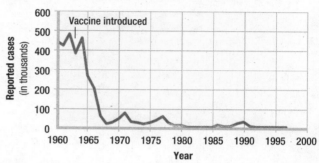

Reported Cases of Measles, United States, 1960–1996

Source: U.S. Department of Health and Human Services

6 Compare How many cases of measles were reported in the United States in 1962, the year before the measles vaccine was licensed? How many cases were reported 5 years later?

_____

_____

7 Infer How many cases of measles would you predict were reported last year?

_____

8 Hypothesize How can infectious and noninfectious diseases affect personal health?

_____

_____

_____

_____

_____

9 Apply Why might the risk of infectious disease be high in a community that has no water treatment facility?

_____

_____

_____

_____

My Notes

Nutrition and Fitness

ESSENTIAL QUESTION

How are nutrition, fitness, and health related?

By the end of this lesson, you should be able to explain how healthy habits such as eating proper nutrients and staying physically fit can help a person live a healthy lifestyle.

Exercise such as playing basketball is one way to stay fit and healthy.

 Engage Your Brain

1 **Explain** Draw a picture of a balanced meal. Label the foods and drinks that are part of the meal. Write a caption that explains why this meal is balanced.

_____

_____

_____

2 **Predict.** Which food group is pictured above? Which nutrient do you think this food group provides?

_____

_____

_____

Active Reading

3 **Synthesize** Many English words have their roots in other languages. Use the Latin words below to make an educated guess about the meaning of the words *nutrient* and *diet*.

Latin word	Meaning
nutrire	to nourish, help grow
diaeta	manner of living

Example sentence
Fruits and vegetables are good snacks because they contain many <u>nutrients</u>.

nutrient:

_____

_____

Example sentence
In Japan, many people eat a <u>diet</u> that includes fish.

diet:

_____

_____

Vocabulary Terms

- nutrition
- nutrient
- diet
- overweight
- obesity
- eating disorder
- physical fitness

4 **Identify** This list contains the key terms that you'll learn in this lesson. As you read, circle the definition of each term.

Nutrient Power

What are the six classes of nutrients?

Have you heard the phrase "You are what you eat"? It's the idea that the food you eat affects your health. **Nutrition** (noo•TRISH•uhn) is the study of food and the ways in which the body uses food. The body gets nutrients from food. A **nutrient** (NOO•tree•uhnt) is a substance that provides energy or helps form body tissues. Nutrients are necessary for life and growth. The six classes of nutrients are carbohydrates, proteins, fats, vitamins, minerals, and water.

> **Active Reading** 5 **Identify** As you read, underline the function of carbohydrates in the body.

Carbohydrates

Simple carbohydrates, such as table sugar and honey, are made up of one or two sugar molecules. These sugars give you quick energy. Complex carbohydrates, such as bread and grain products, are made up of many sugar molecules and give you long-lasting energy. Fiber is a complex carbohydrate that aids digestion. Whole grains, fruits, and vegetables contain fiber.

Proteins

Proteins are nutrients used to build, regulate, and repair your body. They are also a source of energy. Your muscles, skin, blood, and all of your tissues contain protein. Proteins are made up of amino acids. When you eat foods containing protein, such as poultry, fish, milk, beans, and eggs, your body breaks the protein down into amino acids. It then uses these amino acids to make the particular proteins your body needs.

6 Identify List at least four foods you have eaten recently that contain protein.

_____

_____

Fats

Fats are used by the body as a source of energy and as a way to store it. Fats contain more energy than carbohydrates and proteins. Fats also store and transport some vitamins, produce hormones, and make cell membranes. While fats are necessary, eating too much can increase your risk of cardiovascular disease. Meat, dairy products, vegetable oils, butter, and fish are all sources of fat.

Water

Did you know that water makes up about 60% of your body? It is found inside and around your cells. Even your blood is mostly water. Water is needed for nearly all of the life processes in your body. Humans can survive for many weeks without food but only a few days without water. Your body gets water from drinking it and from juices, soups, milk, fruits, and vegetables.

7 Analyze What are sources of water in your diet?

_____

_____

Vitamins and Minerals

Vitamins are nutrients that help the body carry out specific functions. Many of the vitamins work together with enzymes, which are proteins, to carry out chemical reactions in the body. The body can make some vitamins. Other vitamins can be obtained only from food.

Minerals are chemical elements that are not made by the body. They are required for nervous system function and form important parts of many cell structures. Eating a variety of healthy food will help you get all the vitamins and minerals you need.

Think Outside the Book Inquiry

8 Evaluate What are some of the factors that might influence your food choices when planning a balanced diet? Discuss your answers with a classmate.

Let's Eat!

Reading food labels can help you choose healthful foods.

What can you use to choose a healthful diet?

When you think of the word *diet,* what comes to mind? A person's **diet** is the type and amount of food that a person eats. A healthy diet includes a balance of all the essential nutrients. The levels of nutrients you need depend on your age, sex, and how active you are. Your energy needs also depend on these factors. The amount of energy that you get from food is measured in calories. Most teenage girls need between 1,800 and 2,200 calories per day, and most teenage boys need between 2,200 and 2,800 calories per day.

Active Reading **9 Identify** As you read, underline where you can find the amount of nutrients a packaged food provides.

U.S. Recommended Daily Values

Packaged foods must have Nutrition Facts labels. Nutrition Facts labels show the amounts of certain nutrients in one serving of the food. The labels also tell you how many servings are in the container of food and the serving size. A food package may have more than one serving. The U.S. recommended daily allowances (RDAs) are the recommended nutrient intakes that will meet the needs of most healthy people. A Daily Value is a recommended daily amount of a nutrient. You can tell whether a food is high or low in a nutrient by looking at the percentage of the daily value the food provides for each nutrient listed. The percentage of daily values shown is based on a diet that consists of 2,000 calories per day.

Visualize It!

10 Identify On the food label shown, how many calories are in one serving? What percentage of the daily value of sodium is in one serving?

_____

_____

Nutrition Facts

Serving Size 1 cup (228g)
Servings Per Container 2

Amount Per Serving	
Calories 260	Calories from Fat 120

	% Daily Value*
Total Fat 13g	20%
Saturated Fat 5g	25%
Trans Fat 2g	
Cholesterol 30mg	10%
Sodium 660mg	28%
Potassium 700mg	20%
Total Carbohydrate 31g	10%
Dietary Fiber 0g	0%
Sugars 5g	
Protein 5g	

Vitamin A	4%
Vitamin C	2%
Calcium	15%
Iron	4%

* Percent Daily Values are based on a 2,000 calorie diet. Your Daily Values may be higher or lower depending on your calorie needs.

Check the calories.

Check the % Daily Values.

Limit saturated and trans fats, cholesterol, and sodium.

Get enough potassium, fiber, and vitamins.

MyPlate

The U.S. Department of Agriculture created the MyPlate icon as a tool to help people make healthy food choices. MyPlate shows the relative amount of food from five food groups that a person needs to build a healthy meal. The MyPlate icon reminds people to choose fruits and vegetables as half of a healthy meal. Additional recommendations found at ChooseMyPlate.gov include consuming whole grain foods and switching to fat-free or low-fat (1%) milk. Also found are how many calories you need per day and tips for making food choices for a healthy lifestyle.

 **Visualize It!**

11 List Add a food under each group that you like or have eaten in the past couple of days.

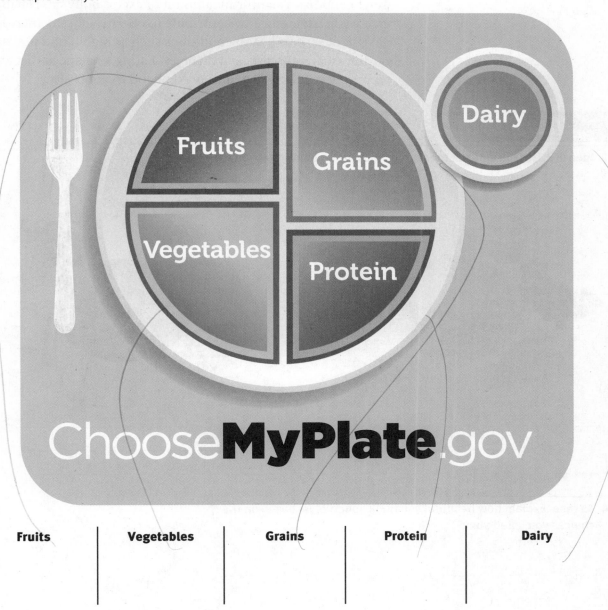

Fruits	Vegetables	Grains	Protein	Dairy

Let's Stay Healthy!

12 Identify As you read, underline the health problems that might result from obesity.

What are the health consequences of poor nutrition?

Health problems can result from eating too much food, not enough food, or not enough of specific nutrients. People who consume too many calories may become *overweight* or suffer from *obesity*. Being **overweight** means a person is heavy for his or her height and has excess stored fat. **Obesity** happens when a person weighs more than 20 percent above his or her recommended body weight and has a significant amount of excess body fat. Having an inactive lifestyle can also contribute to obesity. Obesity increases the risk of serious health conditions such as high blood pressure, cardiovascular disease, and diabetes. Eating a balanced diet and exercising regularly can both prevent and treat obesity.

Visualize It!

13 Identify List the kinds of foods from each group below that you eat.

(A)

_____

_____

_____

(B)

_____

_____

_____

14 Assess Explain how healthful you think your diet is, based on the choices you listed above.

_____

_____

_____

What are eating disorders?

People who do not get enough calories can suffer from starvation or malnutrition. Starvation causes the body to consume its own cells to get energy, which weakens the body. In *malnutrition*, a diet lacks certain nutrients, so the body will not be able to perform certain functions, and serious illnesses may develop. An **eating disorder** is a disease in which a person has an unhealthy concern for his or her body shape and weight.

Anorexia nervosa (an•uh•REK•see•uh ner•VOH•suh) is an eating disorder characterized by self-starvation and an intense fear of gaining weight. *Bulimia* (boo•LEE•me•uh) *nervosa* is characterized by binge eating followed by induced vomiting. Some people suffering from bulimia use laxatives or diuretics to rid their bodies of food and water. Bulimia can damage teeth, the digestive system, and the kidneys. Both anorexia and bulimia can cause weak bones, low blood pressure, and heart problems. These diseases can be fatal if not treated. If you are worried that you or someone you know may have an eating disorder, talk to an adult.

What is the relationship between nutrition and health?

Good nutrition can lead to good health. By eating a balanced diet, drinking water, and getting the right amount of calories, a person can lower cholesterol levels and prevent some diseases. Good nutrition can help you maintain a healthy weight, too. A person who practices healthful eating habits has more energy to do well in both school and physical activities.

Visualize It!

15 Explain Describe how the image below relates nutrition and health.

_____

_____

_____

_____

_____

_____

_____

These athletes are eating healthful snacks after exercising.

Let's Get Fit!

What are the health benefits of exercise?

The ability to perform daily physical activities without becoming short of breath, sore, or overly tired is called **physical fitness**. Physical fitness is an overall state of physical health. Exercise is any physical activity that helps keep you physically fit. Exercise helps to build muscle, strengthen bone, and develop cardiovascular and respiratory endurance.

Brain Exercise reduces stress and helps you relax. People can often focus better after exercising.

Heart and Lungs Exercise helps your heart and lungs work more efficiently, which allows more blood and oxygen to circulate throughout the body.

Blood Vessels Exercise helps control cholesterol and blood-sugar levels. It also controls stress-hormone levels, which helps to prevent heart disease and keeps blood vessels healthy.

Muscles Exercise helps muscles get strong and more flexible. These changes reduce the risk of injury and help prevent muscles from becoming small and weak.

Bones Exercise helps build strong bones and develops coordination in growing adolescents.

The Body Exercise increases your metabolic rate, which helps the body use the food you eat for energy and maintain a healthy weight.

Visualize It!

16 Describe What nutrient is this jogger replenishing in her body as she exercises? Why might it be important to do this?

_____

_____

_____

What are two types of exercise?

Additional information found at ChooseMyPlate.gov recommends that teens get about an hour of moderate or vigorous physical activity every day. Moderate and vigorous activities are exercises that increase your heart rate, such as dancing, weight training, or running. Walking slowly is not intense enough to keep you fit.

Think Outside the Book

17 Apply Make a plan for incorporating exercise into your daily routine.

Aerobic

Aerobic exercise raises the heart and breathing rates. This increases the level of oxygen in muscles, allowing the release of energy from food. Walking briskly, running, and swimming are all examples of aerobic exercise. Aerobic exercise strengthens the heart, lungs, muscles, bones, and immune system. Aerobic exercise burns calories, which helps achieve and keep a healthy weight.

Anaerobic

Anaerobic exercise involves intense muscle activity for a short time. Anaerobic exercise occurs in too short a time for oxygen levels in muscles to be increased. So, muscle cells release energy from food without oxygen. Weight lifting, wrestling, and sprinting are examples of anaerobic exercise. Anaerobic exercise builds muscle mass and increases strength.

Aerobic exercise

Anaerobic exercise

18 Compare How do aerobic exercise and anaerobic exercise differ?

Aerobic exercise	Anaerobic exercise

Visual Summary

To complete this summary, check the box that indicates true or false. Then, use the key below to check your answers. You can use this page to review the main concepts of the lesson.

Nutrients are necessary for energy and growth.

    T   F

19 ☐ ☐ *The body does not need fats or oils.*

Nutrition explains the ways our bodies use food.

    T   F

21 ☐ ☐ *Daily Values are used on food labels to show the food group in which a nutrient belongs.*

MyPlate helps people make healthy food choices.

    T   F

20 ☐ ☐ *Most of the food you eat each day should come from the meat and beans group.*

Exercise contributes to physical fitness.

    T   F

22 ☐ ☐ *Anaerobic exercise builds muscle strength and mass.*

Answers: 19 F; 20 F; 21 F; 22 T

23 Synthesize Explain how both diet and exercise contribute to maintaining a healthy weight.

Lesson Review

Vocabulary

Fill in the blank with the term that best completes the following sentences.

1 There are six classes of _____ the body needs for growth.

2 Being heavy for your height means being _____

3 _____ is the ability to do daily activities without becoming overly tired.

4 Weighing 20% above the recommended weight is called _____

Key Concepts

5 Relate How do eating disorders affect health?

_____

_____

_____

_____

6 Identify What common benefit do proteins, carbohydrates, and fats provide for the body?

_____

_____

_____

7 Describe How does MyPlate help people make healthy choices about what foods to eat?

_____

_____

_____

_____

8 Compare How do aerobic and anaerobic exercise affect the body?

_____

_____

_____

_____

_____

Critical Thinking

Use the photo below to answer the questions.

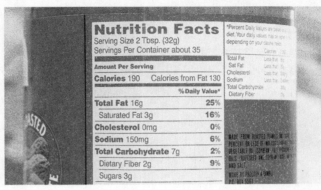

9 Identify What percentage of the Daily Value of carbohydrates is found in a serving of this food?

_____

_____

10 Apply How can food labels be used to choose a healthful diet?

_____

_____

_____

_____

11 Predict How would your health be affected if your diet consistently lacked important nutrients?

_____

_____

_____

_____

12 Analyze Playing soccer involves jogging and sprinting. Explain whether playing soccer is aerobic exercise, anaerobic exercise, or both.

_____

_____

_____

_____

My Notes

Unit 2 ⟨Big Idea⟩ A healthy immune system, good nutrition, and physical activity are all important in the maintenance of the human body.

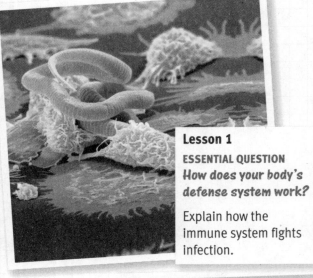

Lesson 1

ESSENTIAL QUESTION
How does your body's defense system work?

Explain how the immune system fights infection.

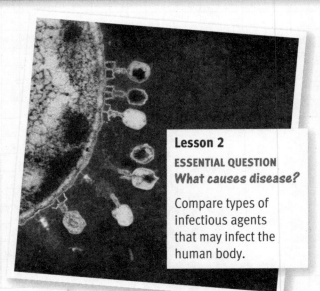

Lesson 2

ESSENTIAL QUESTION
What causes disease?

Compare types of infectious agents that may infect the human body.

Lesson 3

ESSENTIAL QUESTION
How are nutrition, fitness, and health related?

Explain how healthy habits such as eating proper nutrients and staying physically fit can help a person live a healthy lifestyle.

Connect ESSENTIAL QUESTIONS
Lessons 1 and 2

1 Summarize What defenses protect your body against infectious disease?

_____

_____

_____

_____

Think Outside the Book

2 Synthesize Choose one of these activities to help synthesize what you have learned in this unit.

☐ Using what you learned in lessons 1 through 3, create a poster presentation to explain how a balanced diet can help contribute to a healthy immune system.

☐ Using what you learned in lessons 2 and 3, create a brochure that explains why it is important to avoid consuming contaminated water or foods while traveling abroad and what travelers can do to maintain a healthy diet while traveling. Your brochure should cover the terms *nutrition* and *nutrient*.

Unit 2 Review

Name _____

Vocabulary

Check the box to show whether each statement is true or false.

T	F	
☐	☐	**1** A <u>pathogen</u> is an organism, virus, or particle that can make you sick.
☐	☐	**2** An <u>antibody</u> is a substance that causes human cells to mutate.
☐	☐	**3** A <u>noninfectious disease</u> is a disease that can be spread from one person to another.
☐	☐	**4** A <u>nutrient</u> is a substance in food that provides energy or helps build body cells and tissues.
☐	☐	**5** <u>Obesity</u> is the condition of having excess stored fat but weighing less than 20% above the recommended weight range.

Key Concepts

Read each question below, and circle the best answer.

6 All of the students at Lincoln Middle School were given a vaccine. What can you conclude about the students at Lincoln Middle School?

A The students will never get sick again.

B The students were exposed to a noninfectious disease.

C The students must have all had autoimmune disorders.

D The students will be better able to resist the disease the vaccine was for.

7 Which of the following diseases is caused by a virus?

A skin cancer   **C** type 1 diabetes

B influenza   **D** ringworm

8 Which of the following is an immune system disorder?

A allergies   **C** influenza

B strep throat   **D** athlete's foot

9 The pictures below show three types of cells.

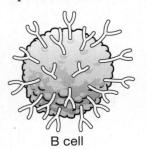
B cell

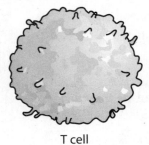
T cell

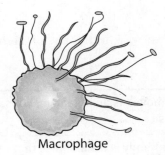
Macrophage

Which of the following is true of these three cells?

A The B cell and T cell are pathogens that the macrophage fights against.

B All three cells are types of white blood cells.

C These are different examples of bacteria.

D These cells cause different types of cancer.

10 Which of the following correctly lists the six classes of nutrients?

A Grains, vegetables, fruits, fats, milk, and meats

B Proteins, grains, minerals, dairy, bread, and oils

C Glucose, fructose, whole grains, refined grains, starches, and fiber

D Carbohydrates, proteins, fats, vitamins, minerals, and water

11 Malik's mother told him that he should go outside and get some more exercise instead of playing video games. Malik said that he already got 30 minutes of activity when he walked to and from school. According to the government's guidelines for a teenager, how much more exercise should Malik try to get today?

A None; Malik is correct that 30 minutes a day is the recommended amount.

B 15 more minutes

C 30 more minutes

D 60 more minutes

12 The pictures below show three pathogens and label a disease they may cause.

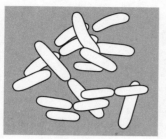

Tuberculosis

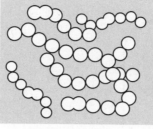

Strep throat

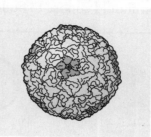

Common cold

Which of the following sets of these diseases could be treated by antibiotics?

A tuberculosis and common cold

B common cold and strep throat

C strep throat, common cold, and tuberculosis

D strep throat and tuberculosis

Critical Thinking

Answer the following questions in the space provided.

13 On a quiz, Keisha was given a list of terms that describe the human body's defenses against infection. The terms were to be placed in a table to classify them as external or internal defenses. She has already placed most of the terms in the table, but still needs to place the terms *macrophage* and *mucus*. Write the terms macrophage and mucus under the proper column in the table.

External Defenses	Internal Defenses
Hair	Fever
Skin	Inflammation
Oil	T cells
Fingernails	B cells
Tears	

Explain how the body's external defenses help to prevent diseases.

_____

_____

_____

_____

14 The MyPlate diagram shown below identifies the major food groups and how much of each you should choose to build a healthy meal.

Fill in the food groups that are missing from the MyPlate icon above.
Then describe a healthy lunch for yourself and how it draws from the MyPlate food groups.

_____

_____

_____

_____

Connect **ESSENTIAL QUESTIONS**
Lessons 1, 2, and 3

Answer the following question in the space provided.

15 Areas that are hit by natural disasters and where food and water become scarce, will often also have problems with infectious diseases. Use what you learned in lessons 1 through 3 to explain how infection might spread, how people fight off diseases, and why malnutrition can lead to the spread of disease.

_____

_____

_____

_____

_____

_____

_____

Look It Up!

References

Mineral Properties

Here are five steps to take in mineral identification:

1 Determine the color of the mineral. Is it light-colored, dark-colored, or a specific color?

2 Determine the luster of the mineral. Is it metallic or non-metallic?

3 Determine the color of any powder left by its streak.

4 Determine the hardness of your mineral. Is it soft, hard, or very hard? Using a glass plate, see if the mineral scratches it.

5 Determine whether your sample has cleavage or any special properties.

TERMS TO KNOW	DEFINITION
adamantine	a non-metallic luster like that of a diamond
cleavage	how a mineral breaks when subject to stress on a particular plane
luster	the state or quality of shining by reflecting light
streak	the color of a mineral when it is powdered
submetallic	between metallic and nonmetallic in luster
vitreous	glass-like type of luster

Silicate Minerals					
Mineral	**Color**	**Luster**	**Streak**	**Hardness**	**Cleavage and Special Properties**
Beryl	deep green, pink, white, bluish green, or yellow	vitreous	white	7.5–8	1 cleavage direction; some varieties fluoresce in ultraviolet light
Chlorite	green	vitreous to pearly	pale green	2–2.5	1 cleavage direction
Garnet	green, red, brown, black	vitreous	white	6.5–7.5	no cleavage
Hornblende	dark green, brown, or black	vitreous	none	5–6	2 cleavage directions
Muscovite	colorless, silvery white, or brown	vitreous or pearly	white	2–2.5	1 cleavage direction
Olivine	olive green, yellow	vitreous	white or none	6.5–7	no cleavage
Orthoclase	colorless, white, pink, or other colors	vitreous	white or none	6	2 cleavage directions
Plagioclase	colorless, white, yellow, pink, green	vitreous	white	6	2 cleavage directions
Quartz	colorless or white; any color when not pure	vitreous or waxy	white or none	7	no cleavage

Nonsilicate Minerals

Mineral	Color	Luster	Streak	Hardness	Cleavage and Special Properties
Native Elements					
Copper	copper-red	metallic	copper-red	2.5–3	no cleavage
Diamond	pale yellow or colorless	adamantine	none	10	4 cleavage directions
Graphite	black to gray	submetallic	black	1–2	1 cleavage direction
Carbonates					
Aragonite	colorless, white, or pale yellow	vitreous	white	3.5–4	2 cleavage directions; reacts with hydrochloric acid
Calcite	colorless or white to tan	vitreous	white	3	3 cleavage directions; reacts with weak acid; double refraction
Halides					
Fluorite	light green, yellow, purple, bluish green, or other colors	vitreous	none	4	4 cleavage directions; some varieties fluoresce
Halite	white	vitreous	white	2.0–2.5	3 cleavage directions
Oxides					
Hematite	reddish brown to black	metallic to earthy	dark red to red-brown	5.6–6.5	no cleavage; magnetic when heated
Magnetite	iron-black	metallic	black	5.5–6.5	no cleavage; magnetic
Sulfates					
Anhydrite	colorless, bluish, or violet	vitreous to pearly	white	3–3.5	3 cleavage directions
Gypsum	white, pink, gray, or colorless	vitreous, pearly, or silky	white	2.0	3 cleavage directions
Sulfides					
Galena	lead-gray	metallic	lead-gray to black	2.5–2.8	3 cleavage directions
Pyrite	brassy yellow	metallic	greenish, brownish, or black	6–6.5	no cleavage

References

Geologic Time Scale

Geologists developed the geologic time scale to represent the 4.6 billion years of Earth's history that have passed since Earth formed. This scale divides Earth's history into blocks of time. The boundaries between these time intervals (shown in millions of years ago or mya in the table below), represent major changes in Earth's history. Some boundaries are defined by mass extinctions, major changes in Earth's surface, and/or major changes in Earth's climate.

The four major divisions that encompass the history of life on Earth are Precambrian time, the Paleozoic era, the Mesozoic era, and the Cenozoic era. The largest divisions are eons. **Precambrian time** is made up of the first three eons, over 4 billion years of Earth's history.

The **Paleozoic era** lasted from 542 mya to 251 mya. All major plant groups, except flowering plants, appeared during this era. By the end of the era, reptiles, winged insects, and fishes had also appeared. The largest known mass extinction occurred at the end of this era.

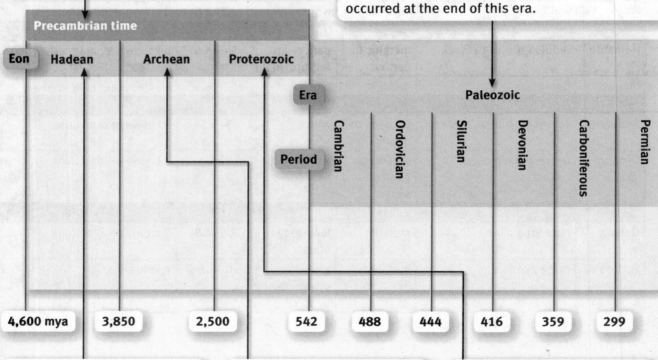

The **Hadean eon** lasted from about 4.6 billion years ago (bya) to 3.85 bya. It is described based on evidence from meteorites and rocks from the moon.

The **Archean eon** lasted from 3.85 bya to 2.5 bya. The earliest rocks from Earth that have been found and dated formed at the start of this eon.

The **Proterozoic eon** lasted from 2.5 bya to 542 mya. The first organisms, which were single-celled organisms, appeared during this eon. These organisms produced so much oxygen that they changed Earth's oceans and Earth's atmosphere.

Divisions of Time

The divisions of time shown here represent major changes in Earth's surface and when life developed and changed significantly on Earth. As new evidence is found, the boundaries of these divisions may shift. The Phanerozoic eon is divided into three eras. The beginning of each of these eras represents a change in the types of organisms that dominated Earth. And, each era is commonly characterized by the types of organisms that dominated the era. These eras are divided into periods, and periods are divided into epochs.

The **Mesozoic era** lasted from 251 mya to 65.5 mya. During this era, many kinds of dinosaurs dominated land, and giant lizards swam in the ocean. The first birds, mammals, and flowering plants also appeared during this time. About two-thirds of all land species went extinct at the end of this era.

The **Phanerozoic eon** began 542 mya. We live in this eon.

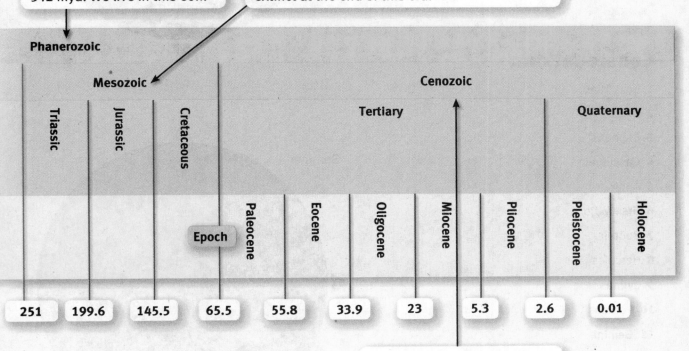

The **Cenozoic era** began 65.5 mya and continues today. Mammals dominate this era. During the Mesozoic era, mammals were small in size but grew much larger during the Cenozoic era. Primates, including humans, appeared during this era.

Star Charts for the Northern Hemisphere

A star chart is a map of the stars in the night sky. It shows the names and positions of constellations and major stars. Star charts can be used to identify constellations and even to orient yourself using Polaris, the North Star.

Because Earth moves through space, different constellations are visible at different times of the year. The star charts on these pages show the constellations visible during each season in the Northern Hemisphere.

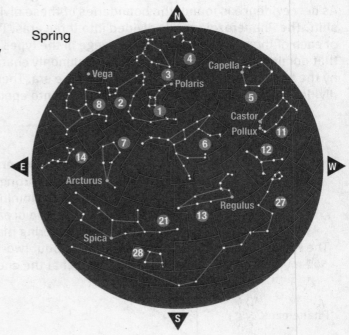

Spring

Constellations

1 Ursa Minor

2 Draco

3 Cepheus

4 Cassiopeia

5 Auriga

6 Ursa Major

7 Boötes

8 Hercules

9 Cygnus

10 Perseus

11 Gemini

12 Cancer

13 Leo

14 Serpens

15 Sagitta

16 Pegasus

17 Pisces

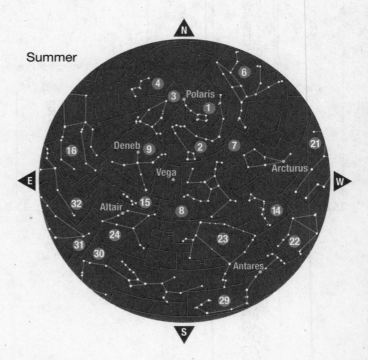

Summer

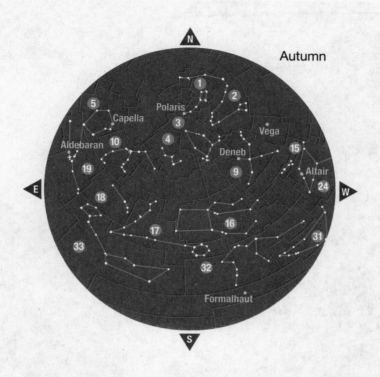

Autumn

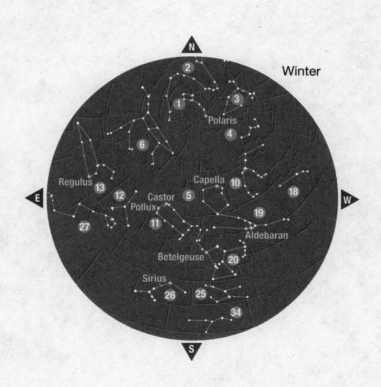

Winter

Constellations

18 Aries

19 Taurus

20 Orion

21 Virgo

22 Libra

23 Ophiuchus

24 Aquila

25 Lepus

26 Canis Major

27 Hydra

28 Corvus

29 Scorpius

30 Sagittarius

31 Capricornus

32 Aquarius

33 Cetus

34 Columba

World Map

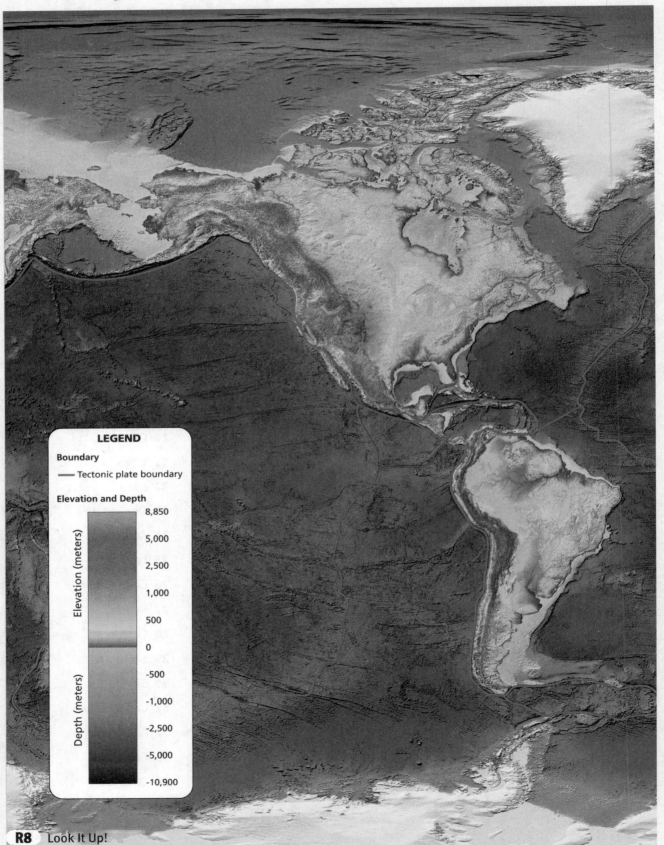

LEGEND

Boundary

— Tectonic plate boundary

Elevation and Depth

Elevation (meters)

8,850
5,000
2,500
1,000
500
0

Depth (meters)

-500
-1,000
-2,500
-5,000
-10,900

References

Classification of Living Things

Domains and Kingdoms

All organisms belong to one of three domains: Domain Archaea, Domain Bacteria, or Domain Eukarya. Some of the groups within these domains are shown below. (Remember that genus names are italicized.)

Domain Archaea

The organisms in this domain are single-celled prokaryotes, many of which live in extreme environments.

Archaea		
Group	**Example**	**Characteristics**
Methanogens	*Methanococcus*	produce methane gas; can't live in oxygen
Thermophiles	*Sulpholobus*	require sulphur; can't live in oxygen
Halophiles	*Halococcus*	live in very salty environments; most can live in oxygen

Domain Bacteria

Organisms in this domain are single-celled prokaryotes and are found in almost every environment on Earth.

Bacteria		
Group	**Example**	**Characteristics**
Bacilli	*Escherichia*	rod shaped; some bacilli fix nitrogen; some cause disease
Cocci	*Streptococcus*	spherical shaped; some cause disease; can form spores
Spirilla	*Treponema*	spiral shaped; cause diseases such as syphilis and Lyme disease

Domain Eukarya

Organisms in this domain are single-celled or multicellular eukaryotes.

Kingdom Protista Many protists resemble fungi, plants, or animals, but are smaller and simpler in structure. Most are single celled.

Protists		
Group	**Example**	**Characteristics**
Sarcodines	*Amoeba*	radiolarians; single-celled consumers
Ciliates	*Paramecium*	single-celled consumers
Flagellates	*Trypanosoma*	single-celled parasites
Sporozoans	*Plasmodium*	single-celled parasites
Euglenas	*Euglena*	single celled; photosynthesize
Diatoms	*Pinnularia*	most are single celled; photosynthesize
Dinoflagellates	*Gymnodinium*	single celled; some photosynthesize
Algae	*Volvox*	single celled or multicellular; photosynthesize
Slime molds	*Physarum*	single celled or multicellular; consumers or decomposers
Water molds	powdery mildew	single celled or multicellular; parasites or decomposers

Kingdom Fungi Most fungi are multicellular. Their cells have thick cell walls. Fungi absorb food from their environment.

Fungi		
Group	**Examples**	**Characteristics**
Threadlike fungi	bread mold	spherical; decomposers
Sac fungi	yeast; morels	saclike; parasites and decomposers
Club fungi	mushrooms; rusts; smuts	club shaped; parasites and decomposers
Lichens	British soldier	a partnership between a fungus and an alga

Kingdom Plantae Plants are multicellular and have cell walls made of cellulose. Plants make their own food through photosynthesis. Plants are classified into divisions instead of phyla.

Plants		
Group	**Examples**	**Characteristics**
Bryophytes	mosses; liverworts	no vascular tissue; reproduce by spores
Club mosses	*Lycopodium;* ground pine	grow in wooded areas; reproduce by spores
Horsetails	rushes	grow in wetland areas; reproduce by spores
Ferns	spleenworts; sensitive fern	large leaves called fronds; reproduce by spores
Conifers	pines; spruces; firs	needlelike leaves; reproduce by seeds made in cones
Cycads	*Zamia*	slow growing; reproduce by seeds made in large cones
Gnetophytes	*Welwitschia*	only three living families; reproduce by seeds
Ginkgoes	*Ginkgo*	only one living species; reproduce by seeds
Angiosperms	all flowering plants	reproduce by seeds made in flowers; fruit

Kingdom Animalia Animals are multicellular. Their cells do not have cell walls. Most animals have specialized tissues and complex organ systems. Animals get food by eating other organisms.

Animals		
Group	**Examples**	**Characteristics**
Sponges	glass sponges	no symmetry or specialized tissues; aquatic
Cnidarians	jellyfish; coral	radial symmetry; aquatic
Flatworms	planaria; tapeworms; flukes	bilateral symmetry; organ systems
Roundworms	*Trichina;* hookworms	bilateral symmetry; organ systems
Annelids	earthworms; leeches	bilateral symmetry; organ systems
Mollusks	snails; octopuses	bilateral symmetry; organ systems
Echinoderms	sea stars; sand dollars	radial symmetry; organ systems
Arthropods	insects; spiders; lobsters	bilateral symmetry; organ systems
Chordates	fish; amphibians; reptiles; birds; mammals	bilateral symmetry; complex organ systems

References

Periodic Table of the Elements

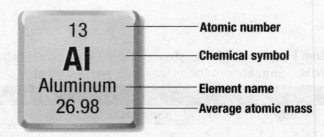

13	Atomic number
Al	Chemical symbol
Aluminum	Element name
26.98	Average atomic mass

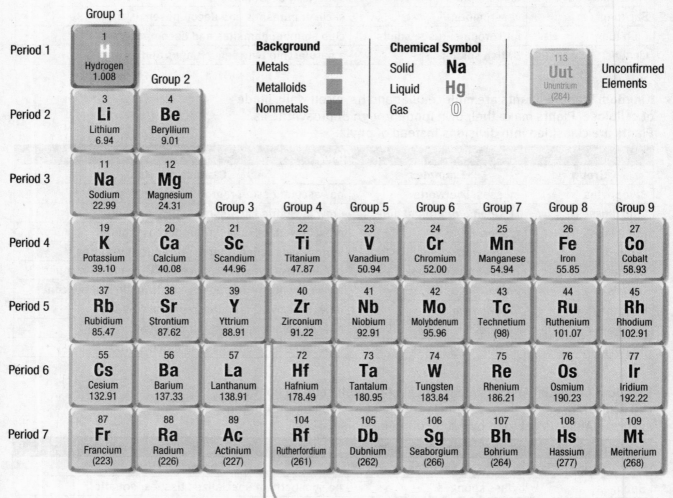

Group 1

Period 1 — 1 **H** Hydrogen 1.008

Background
Metals
Metalloids
Nonmetals

Chemical Symbol
Solid **Na**
Liquid **Hg**
Gas ⓪

113 **Uut** Ununtrium (264) — Unconfirmed Elements

Group 2

Period 2 — 3 **Li** Lithium 6.94 | 4 **Be** Beryllium 9.01

Period 3 — 11 **Na** Sodium 22.99 | 12 **Mg** Magnesium 24.31

Group 3 | **Group 4** | **Group 5** | **Group 6** | **Group 7** | **Group 8** | **Group 9**

Period 4 — 19 **K** Potassium 39.10 | 20 **Ca** Calcium 40.08 | 21 **Sc** Scandium 44.96 | 22 **Ti** Titanium 47.87 | 23 **V** Vanadium 50.94 | 24 **Cr** Chromium 52.00 | 25 **Mn** Manganese 54.94 | 26 **Fe** Iron 55.85 | 27 **Co** Cobalt 58.93

Period 5 — 37 **Rb** Rubidium 85.47 | 38 **Sr** Strontium 87.62 | 39 **Y** Yttrium 88.91 | 40 **Zr** Zirconium 91.22 | 41 **Nb** Niobium 92.91 | 42 **Mo** Molybdenum 95.96 | 43 **Tc** Technetium (98) | 44 **Ru** Ruthenium 101.07 | 45 **Rh** Rhodium 102.91

Period 6 — 55 **Cs** Cesium 132.91 | 56 **Ba** Barium 137.33 | 57 **La** Lanthanum 138.91 | 72 **Hf** Hafnium 178.49 | 73 **Ta** Tantalum 180.95 | 74 **W** Tungsten 183.84 | 75 **Re** Rhenium 186.21 | 76 **Os** Osmium 190.23 | 77 **Ir** Iridium 192.22

Period 7 — 87 **Fr** Francium (223) | 88 **Ra** Radium (226) | 89 **Ac** Actinium (227) | 104 **Rf** Rutherfordium (261) | 105 **Db** Dubnium (262) | 106 **Sg** Seaborgium (266) | 107 **Bh** Bohrium (264) | 108 **Hs** Hassium (277) | 109 **Mt** Meitnerium (268)

Lanthanides — 58 **Ce** Cerium 140.12 | 59 **Pr** Praseodymium 140.91 | 60 **Nd** Neodymium 144.24 | 61 **Pm** Promethium (145) | 62 **Sm** Samarium 150.36

Actinides — 90 **Th** Thorium 232.04 | 91 **Pa** Protactinium 231.04 | 92 **U** Uranium 238.03 | 93 **Np** Neptunium (237) | 94 **Pu** Plutonium (244)

The International Union of Pure and Applied Chemistry (IUPAC) has determined that, because of isotopic variance, the average atomic mass is best represented by a range of values for each of the following elements: hydrogen, lithium, boron, carbon, nitrogen, oxygen, silicon, sulfur, chlorine, and thallium. However, the values in this table are appropriate for everyday calculations.

							Group 18
							2 **He** Helium 4.003

			Group 13	Group 14	Group 15	Group 16	Group 17	
			5 **B** Boron 10.81	6 **C** Carbon 12.01	7 **N** Nitrogen 14.01	8 **O** Oxygen 16.00	9 **F** Fluorine 19.00	10 **Ne** Neon 20.18
			13 **Al** Aluminum 26.98	14 **Si** Silicon 28.09	15 **P** Phosphorus 30.97	16 **S** Sulfur 32.06	17 **Cl** Chlorine 35.45	18 **Ar** Argon 39.95

Group 10	Group 11	Group 12						
28 **Ni** Nickel 58.69	29 **Cu** Copper 63.55	30 **Zn** Zinc 65.38	31 **Ga** Gallium 69.72	32 **Ge** Germanium 72.63	33 **As** Arsenic 74.92	34 **Se** Selenium 78.96	35 **Br** Bromine 79.90	36 **Kr** Krypton 83.80
46 **Pd** Palladium 106.42	47 **Ag** Silver 107.87	48 **Cd** Cadmium 112.41	49 **In** Indium 114.82	50 **Sn** Tin 118.71	51 **Sb** Antimony 121.76	52 **Te** Tellurium 127.60	53 **I** Iodine 126.90	54 **Xe** Xenon 131.29
78 **Pt** Platinum 195.08	79 **Au** Gold 196.97	80 **Hg** Mercury 200.59	81 **Tl** Thallium 204.38	82 **Pb** Lead 207.2	83 **Bi** Bismuth 208.98	84 **Po** Polonium (209)	85 **At** Astatine (210)	86 **Rn** Radon (222)
110 **Ds** Darmstadtium (271)	111 **Rg** Roentgenium (272)	112 **Cn** Copernicium (285)	113 **Uut** Ununtrium (284)	114 **Uuq** Ununquadium (289)	115 **Uup** Ununpentium (288)	116 **Uuh** Ununhexium (292)	117 **Uus** Ununseptium (294)	118 **Uuo** Ununoctium (294)

63 **Eu** Europium 151.96	64 **Gd** Gadolinium 157.25	65 **Tb** Terbium 158.93	66 **Dy** Dysprosium 162.50	67 **Ho** Holmium 164.93	68 **Er** Erbium 167.26	69 **Tm** Thulium 168.93	70 **Yb** Ytterbium 173.05	71 **Lu** Lutetium 174.97
95 **Am** Americium (243)	96 **Cm** Curium (247)	97 **Bk** Berkelium (247)	98 **Cf** Californium (251)	99 **Es** Einsteinium (252)	100 **Fm** Fermium (257)	101 **Md** Mendelevium (258)	102 **No** Nobelium (259)	103 **Lr** Lawrencium (262)

References

Physical Science Refresher

Atoms and Elements

Every object in the universe is made of matter. **Matter** is anything that takes up space and has mass. All matter is made of atoms. An **atom** is the smallest particle into which an element can be divided and still be the same element. An **element**, in turn, is a substance that cannot be broken down into simpler substances by chemical means. Each element consists of only one kind of atom. An element may be made of many atoms, but they are all the same kind of atom.

Atomic Structure

Atoms are made of smaller particles called **electrons, protons,** and **neutrons.** Electrons have a negative electric charge, protons have a positive charge, and neutrons have no electric charge. Together, protons and neutrons form the **nucleus,** or small dense center, of an atom. Because protons are positively charged and neutrons are neutral, the nucleus has a positive charge. Electrons move within an area around the nucleus called the **electron cloud.** Electrons move so quickly that scientists cannot determine their exact speeds and positions at the same time.

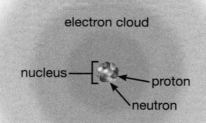

electron cloud

nucleus — proton

neutron

Atomic Number

To help distinguish one element from another, scientists use the atomic numbers of atoms. The **atomic number** is the number of protons in the nucleus of an atom. The atoms of a certain element always have the same number of protons.

When atoms have an equal number of protons and electrons, they are uncharged, or electrically neutral. The atomic number equals the number of electrons in an uncharged atom. The number of neutrons, however, can vary for a given element. Atoms of the same element that have different numbers of neutrons are called **isotopes**.

Periodic Table of the Elements

In the periodic table, each element in the table is in a separate box. And the elements are arranged from left to right in order of increasing atomic number. That is, an uncharged atom of each element has one more electron and one more proton than an uncharged atom of the element to its left. Each horizontal row of the table is called a **period**. Changes in chemical properties of elements across a period correspond to changes in the electron arrangements of their atoms.

Each vertical column of the table is known as a **group.** A group lists elements with similar physical and chemical properties. For this reason, a group is also sometimes called a family. The elements in a group have similar properties because their atoms have the same number of electrons in their outer energy level. For example, the elements helium, neon, argon, krypton, xenon, and radon all have similar properties and are known as the noble gases.

Molecules and Compounds

When two or more elements join chemically, they form a **compound**. A compound is a new substance with properties different from those of the elements that compose it. For example, water, H_2O, is a compound formed when hydrogen (H) and oxygen (O) combine. The smallest complete unit of a compound that has the properties of that compound is called a **molecule**. A chemical formula indicates the elements in a compound. It also indicates the relative number of atoms of each element in the compound. The chemical formula for water is H_2O. So, each water molecule consists of two atoms of hydrogen and one atom of oxygen. The subscript number after the symbol for an element shows how many atoms of that element are in a single molecule of the compound.

Chemical Equations

A chemical reaction occurs when a chemical change takes place. A chemical equation describes a chemical reaction using chemical formulas. The equation indicates the substances that react and the substances that are produced. For example, when carbon and oxygen combine, they can form carbon dioxide, shown in the equation below: $C + O_2 \longrightarrow CO_2$

Acids, Bases, and pH

An **ion** is an atom or group of chemically bonded atoms that has an electric charge because it has lost or gained one or more electrons. When an acid, such as hydrochloric acid, HCl, is mixed with water, it separates into ions. An **acid** is a compound that produces hydrogen ions, H^+, in water. The hydrogen ions then combine with a water molecule to form a hydronium ion, H_3O^+. A **base**, on the other hand, is a substance that produces hydroxide ions, OH^-, in water.

To determine whether a solution is acidic or basic, scientists use pH. The **pH** of a solution is a measure of the hydronium ion concentration in a solution. The pH scale ranges from 0 to 14. Acids have a pH that is less than 7. The lower the number, the more acidic the solution. The middle point, pH = 7, is neutral, neither acidic nor basic. Bases have a pH that is greater than 7. The higher the number is, the more basic the solution.

The pH of Some Common Materials

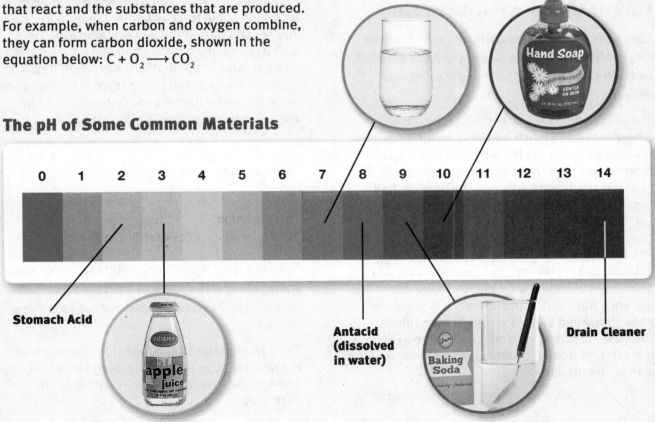

| 0 | 1 | 2 | 3 | 4 | 5 | 6 | 7 | 8 | 9 | 10 | 11 | 12 | 13 | 14 |

Stomach Acid

apple juice

Hand Soap GENTLE ON SKIN 11.25 FL OZ (332 mL)

Antacid (dissolved in water)

Baking Soda

Drain Cleaner

References

Physical Laws and Useful Equations

Law of Conservation of Mass

Mass cannot be created or destroyed during ordinary chemical or physical changes.

The total mass in a closed system is always the same no matter how many physical changes or chemical reactions occur.

Law of Conservation of Energy

Energy can be neither created nor destroyed.

The total amount of energy in a closed system is always the same. Energy can be changed from one form to another, but all of the different forms of energy in a system always add up to the same total amount of energy, no matter how many energy conversions occur.

Law of Universal Gravitation

All objects in the universe attract each other by a force called gravity. The size of the force depends on the masses of the objects and the distance between the objects.

The first part of the law explains why lifting a bowling ball is much harder than lifting a marble. Because the bowling ball has a much larger mass than the marble does, the amount of gravity between Earth and the bowling ball is greater than the amount of gravity between Earth and the marble.

The second part of the law explains why a satellite can remain in orbit around Earth. The satellite is placed at a carefully calculated distance from Earth. This distance is great enough to keep Earth's gravity from pulling the satellite down, yet small enough to keep the satellite from escaping Earth's gravity and wandering off into space.

Newton's Laws of Motion

Newton's first law of motion states that an object at rest remains at rest, and an object in motion remains in motion at constant speed and in a straight line unless acted on by an unbalanced force.

The first part of the law explains why a football will remain on a tee until it is kicked off or until a gust of wind blows it off. The second part of the law explains why a bike rider will continue moving forward after the bike comes to an abrupt stop. Gravity and the friction of the sidewalk will eventually stop the rider.

Newton's second law of motion states that the acceleration of an object depends on the mass of the object and the amount of force applied.

The first part of the law explains why the acceleration of a 4 kg bowling ball will be greater than the acceleration of a 6 kg bowling ball if the same force is applied to both balls. The second part of the law explains why the acceleration of a bowling ball will be greater if a larger force is applied to the bowling ball. The relationship of acceleration (a) to mass (m) and force (F) can be expressed mathematically by the following equation:

$$acceleration = \frac{force}{mass}, \text{ or } a = \frac{F}{m}$$

This equation is often rearranged to read *force = mass × acceleration*, or $F = m \times a$

Newton's third law of motion states that whenever one object exerts a force on a second object, the second object exerts an equal and opposite force on the first.

This law explains that a runner is able to move forward because the ground exerts an equal and opposite force on the runner's foot after each step.

Average speed

$$average\ speed = \frac{total\ distance}{total\ time}$$

Example:
A bicycle messenger traveled a distance of 136 km in 8 h. What was the messenger's average speed?

$$\frac{136\ km}{8\ h} = 17\ km/h$$

The messenger's average speed was **17 km/h.**

Average acceleration

$$average\ acceleration = \frac{final\ velocity - starting\ velocity}{time\ it\ takes\ to\ change\ velocity}$$

Example:
Calculate the average acceleration of an Olympic 100 m dash sprinter who reached a velocity of 20 m/s south at the finish line. The race was in a straight line and lasted 10 s.

$$\frac{20\ m/s - 0\ m/s}{10\ s} = 2\ m/s/s$$

The sprinter's average acceleration was **2 m/s/s south.**

Net force
Forces in the Same Direction

When forces are in the same direction, add the forces together to determine the net force.

Example:
Calculate the net force on a stalled car that is being pushed by two people. One person is pushing with a force of 13 N northwest, and the other person is pushing with a force of 8 N in the same direction.

$$13\ N + 8\ N = 21\ N$$

The net force is **21 N northwest.**

Forces in Opposite Directions

When forces are in opposite directions, subtract the smaller force from the larger force to determine the net force. The net force will be in the direction of the larger force.

Example:
Calculate the net force on a rope that is being pulled on each end. One person is pulling on one end of the rope with a force of 12 N south. Another person is pulling on the opposite end of the rope with a force of 7 N north.

$$12\ N - 7\ N = 5\ N$$

The net force is **5 N south.**

Pressure

Pressure is the force exerted over a given area. The SI unit for pressure is the pascal. Its symbol is Pa.

$$pressure = \frac{force}{area}$$

Example:
Calculate the pressure of the air in a soccer ball if the air exerts a force of 10 N over an area of 0.5 m^2.

$$pressure = \frac{10N}{0.5\ m^2} = \frac{20N}{m^2} = 20\ Pa$$

The pressure of the air inside the soccer ball is **20 Pa.**

Reading and Study Skills

A How-To Manual for Active Reading

This book belongs to you, and you are invited to write in it. In fact, the book won't be complete until you do. Sometimes you'll answer a question or follow directions to mark up the text. Other times you'll write down your own thoughts. And when you're done reading and writing in the book, the book will be ready to help you review what you learned and prepare for tests.

Active Reading Annotations

Before you read, you'll often come upon an Active Reading prompt that asks you to underline certain words or number the steps in a process. Here's an example.

> **Active Reading**
>
> **12 Identify** In this paragraph, number the sequence of sentences that describe replication.

Marking the text this way is called **annotating,** and your marks are called **annotations.** Annotating the text can help you identify important concepts while you read.

There are other ways that you can annotate the text. You can draw an asterisk (*) by vocabulary terms, mark unfamiliar or confusing terms and information with a question mark (?), and mark main ideas with a double underline. And you can even invent your own marks to annotate the text!

Other Annotating Opportunities

Keep your pencil, pen, or highlighter nearby as you read, so you can make a note or highlight an important point at any time. Here are a few ideas to get you started.

- Notice the headings in red and blue. The blue headings are questions that point to the main idea of what you're reading. The red headings are answers to the questions in the blue ones. Together these headings outline the content of the lesson. After reading a lesson, you could write your own answers to the questions.

- Notice the bold-faced words that are highlighted in yellow. They are highlighted so that you can easily find them again on the page where they are defined. As you read or as you review, challenge yourself to write your own sentence using the bold-faced term.

- Make a note in the margin at any time. You might
  - Ask a "What if" question
  - Comment on what you read
  - Make a connection to something you read elsewhere
  - Make a logical conclusion from the text

Use your own language and abbreviations. Invent a code, such as using circles and boxes around words to remind you of their importance or relation to each other. Your annotations will help you remember your questions for class discussions, and when you go back to the lesson later, you may be able to fill in what you didn't understand the first time you read it. Like a scientist in the field or in a lab, you will be recording your questions and observations for analysis later.

Active Reading Questions

After you read, you'll often come upon Active Reading questions that ask you to think about what you've just read. You'll write your answer underneath the question. Here's an example.

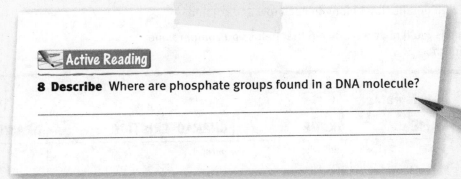

Active Reading

8 Describe Where are phosphate groups found in a DNA molecule?

This type of question helps you sum up what you've just read and pull out the most important ideas from the passage. In this case the question asks you to **describe** the structure of a DNA molecule that you have just read about. Other times you may be asked to do such things as **apply** a concept, **compare** two concepts, **summarize** a process, or **identify a cause-and-effect** relationship. You'll be strengthening those critical thinking skills that you'll use often in learning about science.

Reading and Study Skills

Using Graphic Organizers to Take Notes

Graphic organizers help you remember information as you read it for the first time and as you study it later. There are dozens of graphic organizers to choose from, so the first trick is to choose the one that's best suited to your purpose. Following are some graphic organizers to use for different purposes.

To remember lots of information	To relate a central idea to subordinate details	To describe a process	To make a comparison
• Arrange data in a Content Frame • Use Combination Notes to describe a concept in words and pictures	• Show relationships with a Mind Map or a Main Idea Web • Sum up relationships among many things with a Concept Map	• Use a Process Diagram to explain a procedure • Show a chain of events and results in a Cause-and-Effect Chart	• Compare two or more closely related things in a Venn Diagram

Content Frame

1 Make a four-column chart.

2 Fill the first column with categories (e.g., snail, ant, earthworm) and the first row with descriptive information (e.g., group, characteristic, appearance).

3 Fill the chart with details that belong in each row and column.

4 When you finish, you'll have a study aid that helps you compare one category to another.

Invertebrates

NAME	GROUP	CHARACTERISTICS	DRAWING
snail	mollusks	mangle	
ant	arthropods	six legs, exoskeleton	
earthworm	segmented worms	segmented body, circulatory and digestive systems	
heartworm	roundworms	digestive system	
sea star	echinoderms	spiny skin, tube feet	
jellyfish	cnidarians	stinging cells	

Combination Notes

1 Make a two-column chart.

2 Write descriptive words and definitions in the first column.

3 Draw a simple sketch that helps you remember the meaning of the term in the second column.

NOTES

Types of Forces
• contact force
• gravity
• friction

forces on a box being pushed

contact force

gravity

friction

Mind Map

1 Draw an oval, and inside it write a topic to analyze.

2 Draw two or more arms extending from the oval. Each arm represents a main idea about the topic.

3 Draw lines from the arms on which to write details about each of the main ideas.

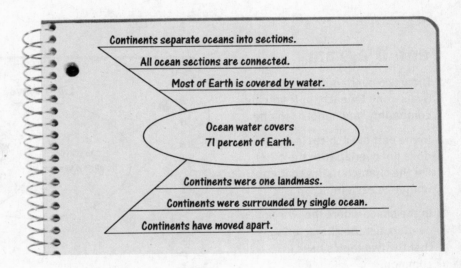

Continents separate oceans into sections.

All ocean sections are connected.

Most of Earth is covered by water.

Ocean water covers 71 percent of Earth.

Continents were one landmass.

Continents were surrounded by single ocean.

Continents have moved apart.

Main Idea Web

1 Make a box and write a concept you want to remember inside it.

2 Draw boxes around the central box, and label each one with a category of information about the concept (e.g., definition, formula, descriptive details).

3 Fill in the boxes with relevant details as you read.

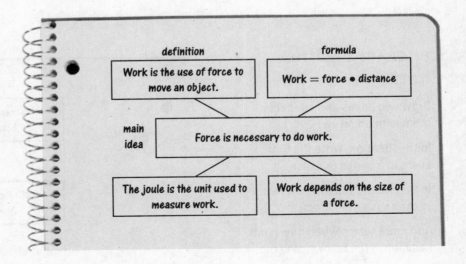

definition

Work is the use of force to move an object.

formula

Work = force • distance

main idea

Force is necessary to do work.

The joule is the unit used to measure work.

Work depends on the size of a force.

Reading and Study Skills

Concept Map

1 Draw a large oval, and inside it write a major concept.

2 Draw an arrow from the concept to a smaller oval, in which you write a related concept.

3 On the arrow, write a verb that connects the two concepts.

4 Continue in this way, adding ovals and arrows in a branching structure, until you have explained as much as you can about the main concept.

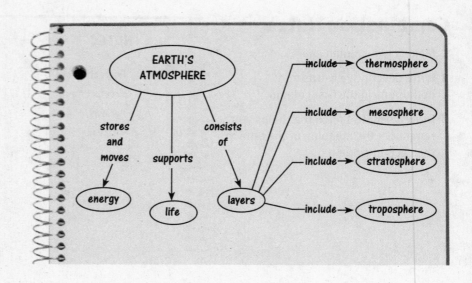

Venn Diagram

1 Draw two overlapping circles or ovals—one for each topic you are comparing—and label each one.

2 In the part of each circle that does not overlap with the other, list the characteristics that are unique to each topic.

3 In the space where the two circles overlap, list the characteristics that the two topics have in common.

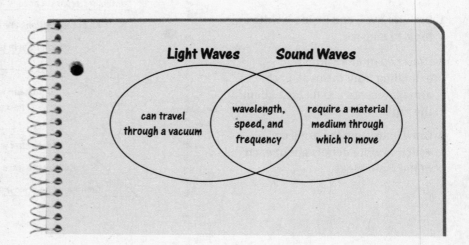

Cause-and-Effect Chart

1 Draw two boxes and connect them with an arrow.

2 In the first box, write the first event in a series (a cause).

3 In the second box, write a result of the cause (the effect).

4 Add more boxes when one event has many effects, or vice versa.

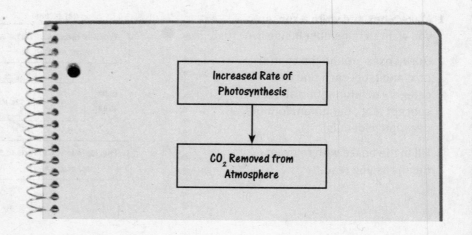

Process Diagram

A process can be a never-ending cycle. As you can see in this technology design process, engineers may backtrack and repeat steps, they may skip steps entirely, or they may repeat the entire process before a useable design is achieved.

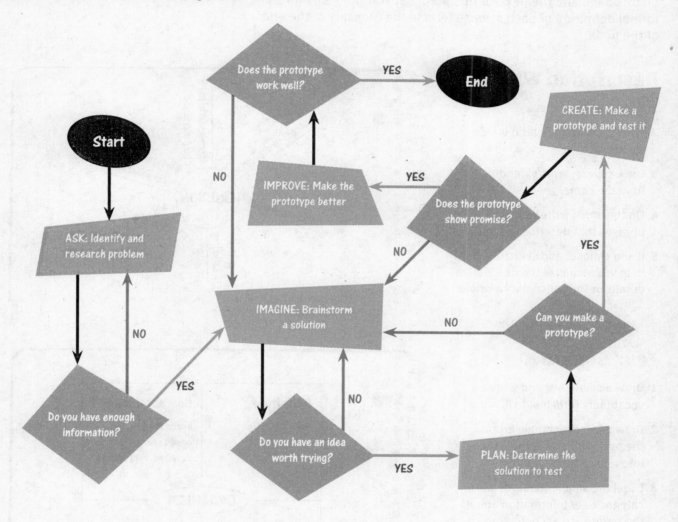

Reading and Study Skills

Using Vocabulary Strategies

Important science terms are highlighted where they are first defined in this book. One way to remember these terms is to take notes and make sketches when you come to them. Use the strategies on this page and the next for this purpose. You will also find a formal definition of each science term in the Glossary at the end of the book.

Description Wheel

1 Draw a small circle.

2 Write a vocabulary term inside the circle.

3 Draw several arms extending from the circle.

4 On the arms, write words and phrases that describe the term.

5 If you choose, add sketches that help you visualize the descriptive details or the concept as a whole.

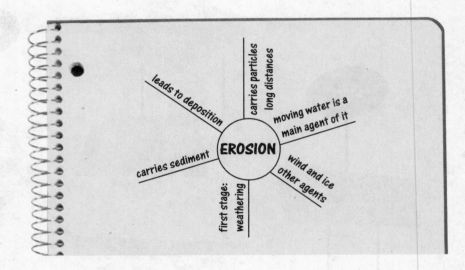

Four Square

1 Draw a small oval and write a vocabulary term inside it.

2 Draw a large rectangle around the oval, and divide the rectangle into four smaller squares.

3 Label the smaller squares with categories of information about the term, such as: definition, characteristics, examples, non-examples, appearance, and root words.

4 Fill the squares with descriptive words and drawings that will help you remember the overall meaning of the term and its essential details.

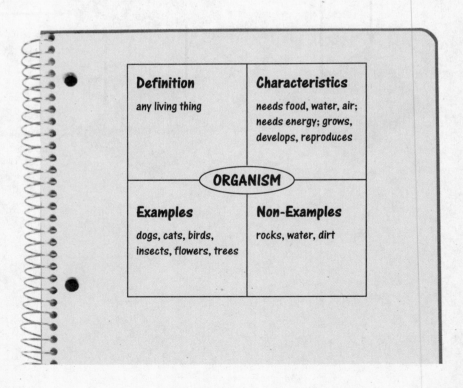

Frame Game

1. Draw a small rectangle, and write a vocabulary term inside it.

2. Draw a larger rectangle around the smaller one. Connect the corners of the larger rectangle to the corners of the smaller one, creating four spaces that frame the word.

3. In each of the four parts of the frame, draw or write details that help define the term. Consider including a definition, essential characteristics, an equation, examples, and a sentence using the term.

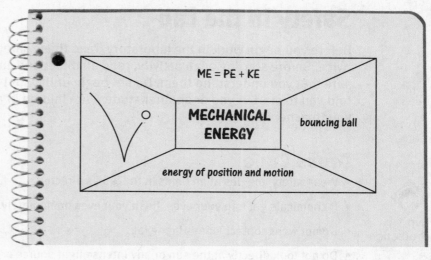

ME = PE + KE

MECHANICAL ENERGY

bouncing ball

energy of position and motion

Magnet Word

1. Draw horseshoe magnet, and write a vocabulary term inside it.

2. Add lines that extend from the sides of the magnet.

3. Brainstorm words and phrases that come to mind when you think about the term.

4. On the lines, write the words and phrases that describe something essential about the term.

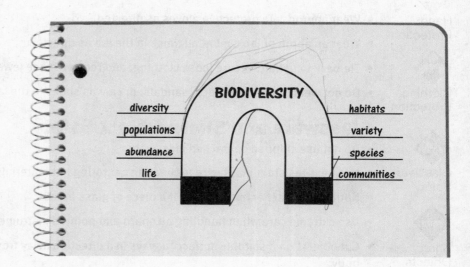

BIODIVERSITY

diversity

populations

abundance

life

habitats

variety

species

communities

Word Triangle

1. Draw a triangle, and add lines to divide it into three parts.

2. Write a term and its definition in the bottom section of the triangle.

3. In the middle section, write a sentence in which the term is used correctly.

4. In the top section, draw a small picture to illustrate the term.

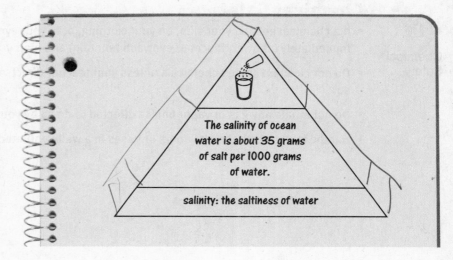

The salinity of ocean water is about 35 grams of salt per 1000 grams of water.

salinity: the saltiness of water

Science Skills

Safety in the Lab

Before you begin work in the laboratory, read these safety rules twice. Before starting a lab activity, read all directions and make sure that you understand them. Do not begin until your teacher has told you to start. If you or another student are injured in any way, tell your teacher immediately.

Dress Code

Eye Protection

Hand Protection

- Wear safety goggles at all times in the lab as directed.
- If chemicals get into your eyes, flush your eyes immediately.
- Do not wear contact lenses in the lab.
- Do not look directly at the sun or any intense light source or laser.
- Do not cut an object while holding the object in your hand.
- Wear appropriate protective gloves as directed.
- Wear an apron or lab coat at all times in the lab as directed.
- Tie back long hair, secure loose clothing, and remove loose jewelry.
- Do not wear open-toed shoes, sandals, or canvas shoes in the lab.

Clothing Protection

Glassware and Sharp Object Safety

Glassware Safety

Sharp Objects Safety

- Do not use chipped or cracked glassware.
- Use heat-resistant glassware for heating or storing hot materials.
- Notify your teacher immediately if a piece of glass breaks.
- Use extreme care when handling all sharp and pointed instruments.
- Cut objects on a suitable surface, always in a direction away from your body.

Chemical Safety

Chemical Safety

- If a chemical gets on your skin, on your clothing, or in your eyes, rinse it immediately (shower, faucet or eyewash fountain) and alert your teacher.
- Do not clean up spilled chemicals unless your teacher directs you to do so.
- Do not inhale any gas or vapor unless directed to do so by your teacher.
- Handle materials that emit vapors or gases in a well-ventilated area.

Electrical Safety

Electrical Safety

- Do not use equipment with frayed electrical cords or loose plugs.

- Do not use electrical equipment near water or when clothing or hands are wet.

- Hold the plug housing when you plug in or unplug equipment.

Heating and Fire Safety

Heating Safety

- Be aware of any source of flames, sparks, or heat (such as flames, heating coils, or hot plates) before working with any flammable substances.

- Know the location of lab fire extinguishers and fire-safety blankets.

- Know your school's fire-evacuation routes.

- If your clothing catches on fire, walk to the lab shower to put out the fire.

- Never leave a hot plate unattended while it is turned on or while it is cooling.

- Use tongs or appropriate insulated holders when handling heated objects.

- Allow all equipment to cool before storing it.

Wafting

Plant and Animal Safety

Plant Safety

- Do not eat any part of a plant.

- Do not pick any wild plants unless your teacher instructs you to do so.

Animal Safety

- Handle animals only as your teacher directs.

- Treat animals carefully and respectfully.

- Wash your hands thoroughly after handling any plant or animal.

Cleanup

Proper Waste Disposal

- Clean all work surfaces and protective equipment as directed by your teacher.

- Dispose of hazardous materials or sharp objects only as directed by your teacher.

Hygienic Care

- Keep your hands away from your face while you are working on any activity.

- Wash your hands thoroughly before you leave the lab or after any activity.

Science Skills

Designing, Conducting, and Reporting an Experiment

An experiment is an organized procedure to study something under specific conditions. Use the following steps of the scientific method when designing or conducting a controlled experiment.

1 Identify a Research Problem

Every day, you make observations by using your senses to gather information. Careful observations lead to good questions, and good questions can lead you to an experiment. Imagine, for example, that you pass a pond every day on your way to school, and you notice green scum beginning to form on top of it. You wonder what it is and why it seems to be growing. You list your questions, and then you do a little research to find out what is already known. A good place to start a research project is at the library. A library catalog lists all of the resources available to you at that library and often those found elsewhere. Begin your search by using:

- keywords or main topics.

- similar words, or synonyms, of your keyword.

The types of resources that will be helpful to you will depend on the kind of information you are interested in. And, some resources are more reliable for a given topic than others. Some different kinds of useful resources are:

- magazines and journals (or periodicals)—articles on a topic.

- encyclopedias—a good overview of a topic.

- books on specific subjects—details about a topic.

- newspapers—useful for current events.

The Internet can also be a great place to find information. Some of your library's reference materials may even be online. When using the Internet, however, it is especially important to make sure you are using appropriate and reliable sources. Websites of universities and government agencies are usually more accurate and reliable than websites created by individuals or businesses. Decide which sources are relevant and reliable for your topic. If in doubt, check with your teacher.

Take notes as you read through the information in these resources. You will probably come up with many questions and ideas for which you can do more research as needed. Once you feel you have enough information, think about the questions you have on the topic. Then, write down the problem that you want to investigate. Your notes might look like these.

© Houghton Mifflin Harcourt Publishing Company

Research Questions	Research Problem	Library and Internet Resources
• How do algae grow? • How do people measure algae? • What kind of fertilizer would affect the growth of algae? • Can fertilizer and algae be used safely in a lab? How?	How does fertilizer affect the algae in a pond?	Pond fertilization: initiating an algal bloom – from University of California Davis website. Blue-Green algae in Wisconsin waters-from the Department of Natural Resources of Wisconsin website.

As you gather information from reliable sources, record details about each source, including author name(s), title, date of publication, and/or web address. Make sure to also note the specific information that you use from each source. Staying organized in this way will be important when you write your report and create a bibliography or works cited list. Recording this information and staying organized will help you credit the appropriate author(s) for the information that you have gathered.

Representing someone else's ideas or work as your own, (without giving the original author credit), is known as plagiarism. Plagiarism can be intentional or unintentional. The best way to make sure that you do not commit plagiarism is to always do your own work and to always give credit to others when you use their words or ideas.

Current scientific research is built on scientific research and discoveries that have happened in the past. This means that scientists are constantly learning from each other and combining ideas to learn more about the natural world through investigation. But, a good scientist always credits the ideas and research that they have gathered from other people to those people. There are more details about crediting sources and creating a bibliography under step 9.

2 Make a Prediction

A prediction is a statement of what you expect will happen in your experiment. Before making a prediction, you need to decide in a general way what you will do in your procedure. You may state your prediction in an if-then format.

Prediction

If the amount of fertilizer in the pond water is increased, then the amount of algae will also increase.

Science Skills

3 Form a Hypothesis

Many experiments are designed to test a hypothesis. A hypothesis is a tentative explanation for an expected result. You have predicted that additional fertilizer will cause additional algae growth in pond water; your hypothesis should state the connection between fertilizer and algal growth.

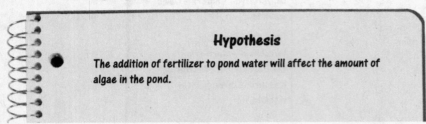

Hypothesis

The addition of fertilizer to pond water will affect the amount of algae in the pond.

4 Identify Variables to Test the Hypothesis

The next step is to design an experiment to test the hypothesis. The experimental results may or may not support the hypothesis. Either way, the information that results from the experiment may be useful for future investigations.

Experimental Group and Control Group

An experiment to determine how two factors are related has a control group and an experimental group. The two groups are the same, except that the investigator changes a single factor in the experimental group and does not change it in the control group.

Experimental Group: two containers of pond water with one drop of fertilizer solution added to each

Control Group: two containers of the same pond water sampled at the same time but with no fertilizer solution added

Variables and Constants

In a controlled experiment, a variable is any factor that can change. Constants are all of the variables that are kept the same in both the experimental group and the control group.

The independent variable is the factor that is manipulated or changed in order to test the effect of the change on another variable. The dependent variable is the factor the investigator measures to gather data about the effect.

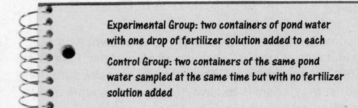

Independent Variable	Dependent Variable	Constants
Amount of fertilizer in pond water	Growth of algae in the pond water	• Where and when the pond water is obtained • The type of container used • Light and temperature conditions where the water is stored

5 Write a Procedure

Write each step of your procedure. Start each step with a verb, or action word, and keep the steps short. Your procedure should be clear enough for someone else to use as instructions for repeating your experiment.

Procedure

1. Use the masking tape and the marker to label the containers with your initials, the date, and the identifiers "Jar 1 with Fertilizer," "Jar 2 with Fertilizer," "Jar 1 without Fertilizer," and "Jar 2 without Fertilizer."

2. Put on your gloves. Use the large container to obtain a sample of pond water.

3. Divide the water sample equally among the four smaller containers.

4. Use the eyedropper to add one drop of fertilizer solution to the two containers labeled, "Jar 1 with Fertilizer," and "Jar 2 with Fertilizer".

5. Cover the containers with clear plastic wrap. Use the scissors to punch ten holes in each of the covers.

6. Place all four containers on a window ledge. Make sure that they all receive the same amount of light.

7. Observe the containers every day for one week.

8. Use the ruler to measure the diameter of the largest clump of algae in each container, and record your measurements daily.

Science Skills

6 Experiment and Collect Data

Once you have all of your materials and your procedure has been approved, you can begin to experiment and collect data. Record both quantitative data (measurements) and qualitative data (observations), as shown below.

Algal Growth and Fertilizer

Date and Time	Experimental Group		Control Group		Observations
	Jar 1 with Fertilizer (diameter of algal clump in mm)	Jar 2 with Fertilizer (diameter of algal clump in mm)	Jar 1 without Fertilizer (diameter of algal clump in mm)	Jar 2 without Fertilizer (diameter of algal clump in mm)	
5/3 4:00 p.m.	0	0	0	0	condensation in all containers
5/4 4:00 p.m.	0	3	0	0	tiny green blobs in Jar 2 with fertilizer
5/5 4:15 p.m.	4	5	0	3	green blobs in Jars 1 and 2 with fertilizer and Jar 2 without fertilizer
5/6 4:00 p.m.	5	6	0	4	water light green in Jar 2 with fertilizer
5/7 4:00 p.m.	8	10	0	6	water light green in Jars 1 and 2 with fertilizer and Jar 2 without fertilizer
5/8 3:30 p.m.	10	18	0	6	cover off of Jar 2 with fertilizer
5/9 3:30 p.m.	14	23	0	8	drew sketches of each container

Drawings of Samples Viewed Under Microscope on 5/9 at 100x

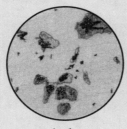

Jar 1 with Fertilizer

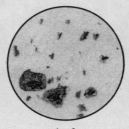

Jar 2 with Fertilizer

Jar 1 without Fertilizer

Jar 2 without Fertilizer

7 Analyze Data

After you complete your experiment, you must analyze all of the data you have gathered. Tables, statistics, and graphs are often used in this step to organize and analyze both the qualitative and quantitative data. Sometimes, your qualitative data are best used to help explain the relationships you see in your quantitative data.

Computer graphing software is useful for creating a graph from data that you have collected. Most graphing software can make line graphs, pie charts, or bar graphs from data that has been organized in a spreadsheet. Graphs are useful for understanding relationships in the data and for communicating the results of your experiment.

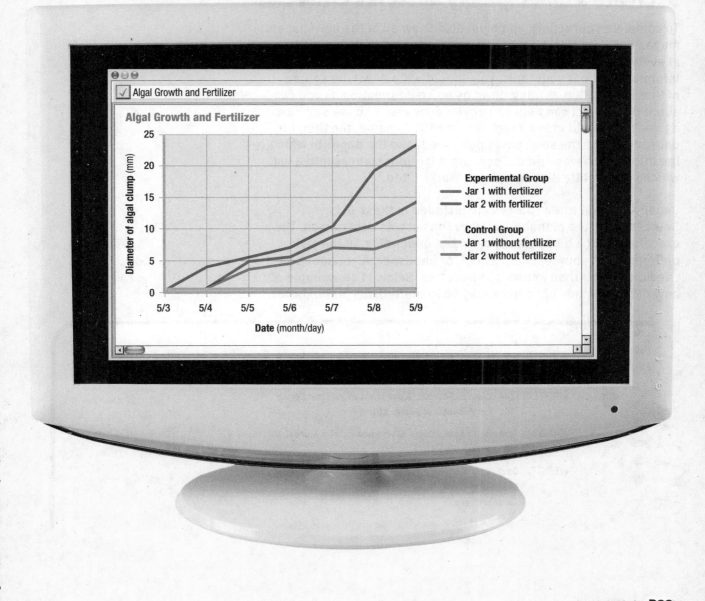

Science Skills

8 Make Conclusions

To draw conclusions from your experiment, first, write your results. Then, compare your results with your hypothesis. Do your results support your hypothesis? What have you learned?

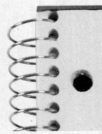

Conclusion

More algae grew in the pond water to which fertilizer had been added than in the pond water to which fertilizer had not been added. My hypothesis was supported. I conclude that it is possible that the growth of algae in ponds can be influenced by the input of fertilizer.

9 Create a Bibliography or Works Cited List

To complete your report, you must also show all of the newspapers, magazines, journals, books, and online sources that you used at every stage of your investigation. Whenever you find useful information about your topic, you should write down the source of that information. Writing down as much information as you can about the subject can help you or someone else find the source again. You should at least record the author's name, the title, the date and where the source was published, and the pages in which the information was found. Then, organize your sources into a list, which you can title Bibliography or Works Cited.

Usually, at least three sources are included in these lists. Sources are listed alphabetically, by the authors' last names. The exact format of a bibliography can vary, depending on the style preferences of your teacher, school, or publisher. Also, books are cited differently than journals or websites. Below is an example of how different kinds of sources may be formatted in a bibliography.

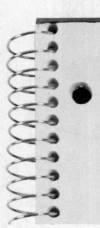

BOOK: Hauschultz, Sara. Freshwater Algae. Brainard, Minnesota: Northwoods Publishing, 2011.

ENCYCLOPEDIA: Lasure, Sedona. "Algae is not all just pond scum." Encyclopedia of Algae. 2009.

JOURNAL: Johnson, Keagan. "Algae as we know it." Sci Journal, vol 64. (September 2010): 201-211.

WEBSITE: Dout, Bill. "Keeping algae scum out of birdbaths." Help Keep Earth Clean. News. January 26, 2011. <www. SaveEarth.org>.

Using a Microscope

Scientists use microscopes to see very small objects that cannot easily be seen with the eye alone. A microscope magnifies the image of an object so that small details may be observed. A microscope that you may use can magnify an object 400 times—the object will appear 400 times larger than its actual size.

Eyepiece Objects are viewed through the eyepiece. The eyepiece contains a lens that commonly magnifies an image ten times.

Body The body separates the lens in the eyepiece from the objective lenses below.

Nosepiece The nosepiece holds the objective lenses above the stage and rotates so that all lenses may be used.

High-Power Objective Lens This is the largest lens on the nosepiece. It magnifies an image approximately 40 times.

Stage The stage supports the object being viewed.

Diaphragm The diaphragm is used to adjust the amount of light passing through the slide and into an objective lens.

Mirror or Light Source Some microscopes use light that is reflected through the stage by a mirror. Other microscopes have their own light sources.

Coarse Adjustment This knob is used to focus the image of an object when it is viewed through the low-power lens.

Fine Adjustment This knob is used to focus the image of an object when it is viewed through the high-power lens.

Low-Power Objective Lens This is the smallest lens on the nosepiece. It magnifies images about 10 times.

Arm The arm supports the body above the stage. Always carry a microscope by the arm and base.

Stage Clip The stage clip holds a slide in place on the stage.

Base The base supports the microscope.

Science Skills

Measuring Accurately

Precision and Accuracy

When you do a scientific investigation, it is important that your methods, observations, and data be both precise and accurate.

Low precision: The darts did not land in a consistent place on the dartboard.

Precision, but not accuracy: The darts landed in a consistent place, but did not hit the bull's eye.

Prescision and accuracy: The darts landed consistently on the bull's eye.

Precision

In science, *precision* is the exactness and consistency of measurements. For example, measurements made with a ruler that has both centimeter and millimeter markings would be more precise than measurements made with a ruler that has only centimeter markings. Another indicator of precision is the care taken to make sure that methods and observations are as exact and consistent as possible. Every time a particular experiment is done, the same procedure should be used. Precision is necessary because experiments are repeated several times and if the procedure changes, the results might change.

Example

Suppose you are measuring temperatures over a two-week period. Your precision will be greater if you measure each temperature at the same place, at the same time of day, and with the same thermometer than if you change any of these factors from one day to the next.

Accuracy

In science, it is possible to be precise but not accurate. *Accuracy* depends on the difference between a measurement and an actual value. The smaller the difference, the more accurate the measurement.

Example

Suppose you look at a stream and estimate that it is about 1 meter wide at a particular place. You decide to check your estimate by measuring the stream with a meter stick, and you determine that the stream is 1.32 meters wide. However, because it is difficult to measure the width of a stream with a meter stick, it turns out that your measurement was not very accurate. The stream is actually 1.14 meters wide. Therefore, even though your estimate of about 1 meter was less precise than your measurement, your estimate was actually more accurate.

Graduated Cylinders

How to Measure the Volume of a Liquid with a Graduated Cylinder

- Be sure that the graduated cylinder is on a flat surface so that your measurement will be accurate.

- When reading the scale on a graduated cylinder, be sure to have your eyes at the level of the surface of the liquid.

- The surface of the liquid will be curved in the graduated cylinder. Read the volume of the liquid at the bottom of the curve, or meniscus (muh-NIHS-kuhs).

- You can use a graduated cylinder to find the volume of a solid object by measuring the increase in a liquid's level after you add the object to the cylinder.

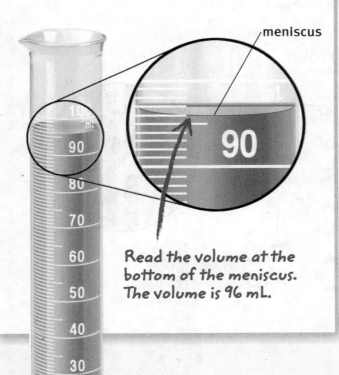

meniscus

Read the volume at the bottom of the meniscus. The volume is 96 mL.

Metric Rulers

How to Measure the Length of a Leaf with a Metric Ruler

1 Lay a ruler flat on top of the leaf so that the 1-centimeter mark lines up with one end. Make sure the ruler and the leaf do not move between the time you line them up and the time you take the measurement.

2 Look straight down on the ruler so that you can see exactly how the marks line up with the other end of the leaf.

3 Estimate the length by which the leaf extends beyond a marking. For example, the leaf below extends about halfway between the 4.2-centimeter and 4.3-centimeter marks, so the apparent measurement is about 4.25 centimeters.

4 Remember to subtract 1 centimeter from your apparent measurement, since you started at the 1-centimeter mark on the ruler and not at the end. The leaf is about 3.25 centimeters long (4.25 cm − 1 cm = 3.25 cm).

Science Skills

Triple Beam Balance

This balance has a pan and three beams with sliding masses, called riders. At one end of the beams is a pointer that indicates whether the mass on the pan is equal to the masses shown on the beams.

How to Measure the Mass of an Object

1 Make sure the balance is zeroed before measuring the mass of an object. The balance is zeroed if the pointer is at zero when nothing is on the pan and the riders are at their zero points. Use the adjustment knob at the base of the balance to zero it.

2 Place the object to be measured on the pan.

3 Move the riders one notch at a time away from the pan. Begin with the largest rider. If moving the largest rider one notch brings the pointer below zero, begin measuring the mass of the object with the next smaller rider.

4 Change the positions of the riders until they balance the mass on the pan and the pointer is at zero. Then add the readings from the three beams to determine the mass of the object.

300 g	position of largest rider
90 g	position of middle rider
+ 3 g	position of smallest rider
393 g	mass of beaker and water

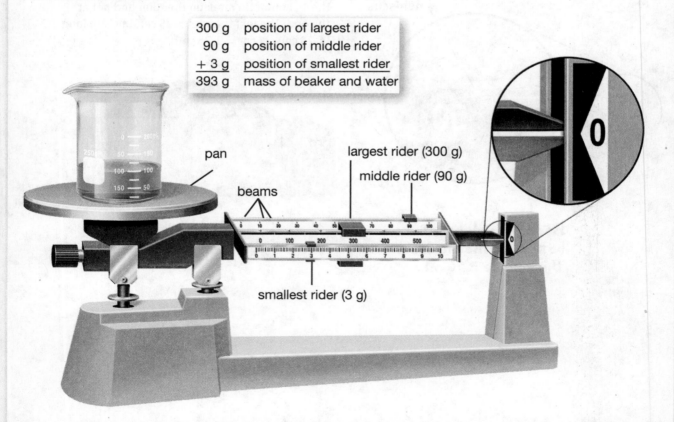

pan

beams

largest rider (300 g)

middle rider (90 g)

smallest rider (3 g)

Using the Metric System and SI Units

Scientists use International System (SI) units for measurements of distance, volume, mass, and temperature. The International System is based on powers of ten and the metric system of measurement.

Basic SI Units		
Quantity	**Name**	**Symbol**
length	meter	m
volume	liter	L
mass	gram	g
temperature	kelvin	K

SI Prefixes		
Prefix	**Symbol**	**Power of 10**
kilo-	k	1000
hecto-	h	100
deca-	da	10
deci-	d	0.1 or $\frac{1}{10}$
centi-	c	0.01 or $\frac{1}{100}$
milli-	m	0.001 or $\frac{1}{1000}$

Changing Metric Units

You can change from one unit to another in the metric system by multiplying or dividing by a power of 10.

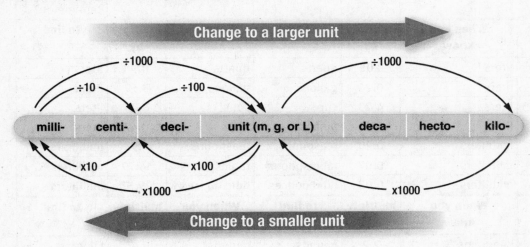

Example

Change 0.64 liters to milliliters.
1 Decide whether to multiply or divide.
2 Select the power of 10.

Change to a smaller unit by multiplying

mL ◄——— x 1000 ——— L

0.64 x 1000 = 640.

ANSWER 0.64 L = 640 mL

Example

Change 23.6 grams to kilograms.
1 Decide whether to multiply or divide.
2 Select the power of 10.

Change to a larger unit by dividing

g ——— ÷ 1000 ———► kg

26.3 ÷ 1000 = 0.0263

ANSWER 23.6 g = 0.0236 kg

Science Skills

Converting Between SI and U.S. Customary Units

Use the chart below when you need to convert between SI units and U.S. customary units.

SI Unit	From SI to U.S. Customary			From U.S. Customary to SI		
Length	**When you know**	**multiply by**	**to find**	**When you know**	**multiply by**	**to find**
kilometer (km) = 1000 m	kilometers	0.62	miles	miles	1.61	kilometers
meter (m) = 100 cm	meters	3.28	feet	feet	0.3048	meters
centimeter (cm) = 10 mm	centimeters	0.39	inches	inches	2.54	centimeters
millimeter (mm) = 0.1 cm	millimeters	0.04	inches	inches	25.4	millimeters
Area	**When you know**	**multiply by**	**to find**	**When you know**	**multiply by**	**to find**
square kilometer (km²)	square kilometers	0.39	square miles	square miles	2.59	square kilometers
square meter (m²)	square meters	1.2	square yards	square yards	0.84	square meters
square centimeter (cm²)	square centimeters	0.155	square inches	square inches	6.45	square centimeters
Volume	**When you know**	**multiply by**	**to find**	**When you know**	**multiply by**	**to find**
liter (L) = 1000 mL	liters	1.06	quarts	quarts	0.95	liters
	liters	0.26	gallons	gallons	3.79	liters
	liters	4.23	cups	cups	0.24	liters
	liters	2.12	pints	pints	0.47	liters
milliliter (mL) = 0.001 L	milliliters	0.20	teaspoons	teaspoons	4.93	milliliters
	milliliters	0.07	tablespoons	tablespoons	14.79	milliliters
	milliliters	0.03	fluid ounces	fluid ounces	29.57	milliliters
Mass	**When you know**	**multiply by**	**to find**	**When you know**	**multiply by**	**to find**
kilogram (kg) = 1000 g	kilograms	2.2	pounds	pounds	0.45	kilograms
gram (g) = 1000 mg	grams	0.035	ounces	ounces	28.35	grams

Temperature Conversions

Even though the kelvin is the SI base unit of temperature, the degree Celsius will be the unit you use most often in your science studies. The formulas below show the relationships between temperatures in degrees Fahrenheit (°F), degrees Celsius (°C), and kelvins (K).

$$°C = \frac{5}{9}\ (°F - 32) \qquad °F = \frac{9}{5}\ °C + 32 \qquad K = °C + 273$$

Examples of Temperature Conversions		
Condition	**Degrees Celsius**	**Degrees Fahrenheit**
Freezing point of water	0	32
Cool day	10	50
Mild day	20	68
Warm day	30	86
Normal body temperature	37	98.6
Very hot day	40	104
Boiling point of water	100	212

Math Refresher

Performing Calculations

Science requires an understanding of many math concepts. The following pages will help you review some important math skills.

Mean

The mean is the sum of all values in a data set divided by the total number of values in the data set. The mean is also called the *average*.

Example

Find the mean of the following set of numbers: 5, 4, 7, and 8.

Step 1   **Find the sum.**

5 + 4 + 7 + 8 = 24

Step 2   **Divide the sum by the number of numbers in your set. Because there are four numbers in this example, divide the sum by 4.**

24 ÷ 4 = 6

Answer **The average, or mean, is 6.**

Median

The median of a data set is the middle value when the values are written in numerical order. If a data set has an even number of values, the median is the mean of the two middle values.

Example

To find the median of a set of measurements, arrange the values in order from least to greatest. The median is the middle value.

13 mm   14 mm   16 mm   21 mm   23 mm

Answer **The median is 16 mm.**

Mode

The mode of a data set is the value that occurs most often.

Example

To find the mode of a set of measurements, arrange the values in order from least to greatest and determine the value that occurs most often.

13 mm, 14 mm, 14 mm, 16 mm,
21 mm, 23 mm, 25 mm

Answer **The mode is 14 mm.**

A data set can have more than one mode or no mode. For example, the following data set has modes of 2 mm and 4 mm:

2 mm   2 mm   3 mm   4 mm   4 mm

The data set below has no mode, because no value occurs more often than any other.

2 mm   3 mm   4 mm   5 mm

Math Refresher

Ratios

A **ratio** is a comparison between numbers, and it is usually written as a fraction.

Example

Find the ratio of thermometers to students if you have 36 thermometers and 48 students in your class.

Step 1   Write the ratio.

$$\frac{36 \text{ thermometers}}{48 \text{ students}}$$

Step 2   Simplify the fraction to its simplest form.

$$\frac{36}{48} = \frac{36 \div 12}{48 \div 12} = \frac{3}{4}$$

The ratio of thermometers to students is **3 to 4** or **3:4**.

Proportions

A **proportion** is an equation that states that two ratios are equal.

$$\frac{3}{1} = \frac{12}{4}$$

To solve a proportion, you can use cross-multiplication. If you know three of the quantities in a proportion, you can use cross-multiplication to find the fourth.

Example

Imagine that you are making a scale model of the solar system for your science project. The diameter of Jupiter is 11.2 times the diameter of the Earth. If you are using a plastic-foam ball that has a diameter of 2 cm to represent the Earth, what must the diameter of the ball representing Jupiter be?

$$\frac{11.2}{1} = \frac{x}{2 \text{ cm}}$$

Step 1   Cross-multiply.

$$\frac{11.2}{1} = \frac{x}{2}$$

$$11.2 \times 2 = x \times 1$$

Step 2   Multiply.

$$22.4 = x \times 1$$

$$x = 22.4 \text{ cm}$$

You will need to use a ball that has a diameter of 22.4 cm to represent Jupiter.

Rates

A **rate** is a ratio of two values expressed in different units. A unit rate is a rate with a denominator of 1 unit.

Example

A plant grew 6 centimeters in 2 days. The plant's rate of growth was $\frac{6 \text{ cm}}{2 \text{ days}}$.

To describe the plant's growth in centimeters per day, write a unit rate.

Divide numerator and denominator by 2:

$$\frac{6 \text{ cm}}{2 \text{ days}} = \frac{6 \text{ cm} \div 2}{2 \text{ days} \div 2}$$

Simplify:
$$= \frac{3 \text{ cm}}{1 \text{ day}}$$

Answer   The plant's rate of growth is 3 centimeters per day.

Percent

A **percent** is a ratio of a given number to 100. For example, 85% = 85/100. You can use percent to find part of a whole.

Example
What is 85% of 40?

Step 1 Rewrite the percent as a decimal by moving the decimal point two places to the left.

$$0.85$$

Step 2 Multiply the decimal by the number that you are calculating the percentage of.

$$0.85 \times 40 = 34$$

85% of 40 is 34.

Decimals

To **add** or **subtract decimals**, line up the digits vertically so that the decimal points line up. Then, add or subtract the columns from right to left. Carry or borrow numbers as necessary.

Example
Add the following numbers: 3.1415 and 2.96.

Step 1 Line up the digits vertically so that the decimal points line up.

$$\begin{array}{r} 3.1415 \\ + 2.96 \\ \hline \end{array}$$

Step 2 Add the columns from right to left, and carry when necessary.

$$\begin{array}{r} 3.1415 \\ + 2.96 \\ \hline 6.1015 \end{array}$$

The sum is 6.1015.

Fractions

A **fraction** is a ratio of two nonzero whole numbers.

Example
Your class has 24 plants. Your teacher instructs you to put 5 plants in a shady spot. What fraction of the plants in your class will you put in a shady spot?

Step 1 In the denominator, write the total number of parts in the whole.

$$\frac{?}{24}$$

Step 2 In the numerator, write the number of parts of the whole that are being considered.

$$\frac{5}{24}$$

So, $\frac{5}{24}$ of the plants will be in the shade.

Math Refresher

Simplifying Fractions

It is usually best to express a fraction in its simplest form. Expressing a fraction in its simplest form is called **simplifying a fraction**.

Example

Simplify the fraction $\frac{30}{45}$ to its simplest form.

Step 1　Find the largest whole number that will divide evenly into both the numerator and denominator. This number is called the greatest common factor (GCF).

Factors of the numerator 30:
1, 2, 3, 5, 6, 10, 15, 30

Factors of the denominator 45:
1, 3, 5, 9, 15, 45

Step 2　Divide both the numerator and the denominator by the GCF, which in this case is 15.

$$\frac{30}{45} = \frac{30 \div 15}{45 \div 15} = \frac{2}{3}$$

Thus, $\frac{30}{45}$ written in its simplest form is $\frac{2}{3}$.

Adding and Subtracting Fractions

To **add** or **subtract fractions** that have the same denominator, simply add or subtract the numerators.

Examples

$\frac{3}{5} + \frac{1}{5} = ?$ and $\frac{3}{4} - \frac{1}{4} = ?$

Step 1　Add or subtract the numerators.

$\frac{3}{5} + \frac{1}{5} = \frac{4}{}$ and $\frac{3}{4} - \frac{1}{4} = \frac{2}{}$

Step 2　Write in the common denominator, which remains the same.

$\frac{3}{5} + \frac{1}{5} = \frac{4}{5}$ and $\frac{3}{4} - \frac{1}{4} = \frac{2}{4}$

Step 3　If necessary, write the fraction in its simplest form.

$\frac{4}{5}$ cannot be simplified, and $\frac{2}{4} = \frac{1}{2}$.

To **add** or **subtract** fractions that have **different denominators,** first find the least common denominator (LCD).

Examples

$\frac{1}{2} + \frac{1}{6} = ?$ and $\frac{3}{4} - \frac{2}{3} = ?$

Step 1　Write the equivalent fractions that have a common denominator.

$\frac{3}{6} + \frac{1}{6} = ?$ and $\frac{9}{12} - \frac{8}{12} = ?$

Step 2　Add or subtract the fractions.

$\frac{3}{6} + \frac{1}{6} = \frac{4}{6}$ and $\frac{9}{12} - \frac{8}{12} = \frac{1}{12}$

Step 3　If necessary, write the fraction in its simplest form.

$\frac{4}{6} = \frac{2}{3}$, and $\frac{1}{12}$ cannot be simplifed.

Multiplying Fractions

To **multiply fractions,** multiply the numerators and the denominators together, and then simplify the fraction to its simplest form.

Example

$\frac{5}{9} \times \frac{7}{10} = ?$

Step 1　Multiply the numerators and denominators.

$$\frac{5}{9} \times \frac{7}{10} = \frac{5 \times 7}{9 \times 10} = \frac{35}{90}$$

Step 2　Simplify the fraction.

$$\frac{35}{90} = \frac{35 \div 5}{90 \div 5} = \frac{7}{18}$$

Dividing Fractions

To **divide fractions**, first rewrite the divisor (the number you divide by) upside down. This number is called the reciprocal of the divisor. Then multiply and simplify if necessary.

Example

$$\frac{5}{8} \div \frac{3}{2} = ?$$

Step 1   Rewrite the divisor as its reciprocal.

$$\frac{3}{2} \rightarrow \frac{2}{3}$$

Step 2   Multiply the fractions.

$$\frac{5}{8} \times \frac{2}{3} = \frac{5 \times 2}{8 \times 3} = \frac{10}{24}$$

Step 3   Simplify the fraction.

$$\frac{10}{24} = \frac{10 \div 2}{24 \div 2} = \frac{5}{12}$$

Using Significant Figures

The **significant figures** in a decimal are the digits that are warranted by the accuracy of a measuring device.

When you perform a calculation with measurements, the number of significant figures to include in the result depends in part on the number of significant figures in the measurements. When you multiply or divide measurements, your answer should have only as many significant figures as the measurement with the fewest significant figures.

Examples

Using a balance and a graduated cylinder filled with water, you determined that a marble has a mass of 8.0 grams and a volume of 3.5 cubic centimeters. To calculate the density of the marble, divide the mass by the volume.

Write the formula for density: $\text{Density} = \dfrac{\text{mass}}{\text{volume}}$

Substitute measurements: $= \dfrac{8.0 \text{ g}}{3.5 \text{ cm}^3}$

Use a calculator to divide: $\approx 2.285714286 \text{ g/cm}^3$

Answer Because the mass and the volume have two significant figures each, give the density to two significant figures. The marble has a density of 2.3 grams per cubic centimeter.

Using Scientific Notation

Scientific notation is a shorthand way to write very large or very small numbers. For example, 73,500,000,000,000,000,000,000 kg is the mass of the moon. In scientific notation, it is 7.35×10^{22} kg. A value written as a number between 1 and 10, times a power of 10, is in scientific notation.

Examples

You can convert from standard form to scientific notation.

Standard Form	Scientific Notation
720,000	7.2×10^5
5 decimal places left	Exponent is 5.
0.000291	2.91×10^{-4}
4 decimal places right	Exponent is −4.

You can convert from scientific notation to standard form.

Scientific Notation	Standard Form
4.63×10^7	46,300,000
Exponent is 7.	7 decimal places right
1.08×10^{-6}	0.00000108
Exponent is −6.	6 decimal places left

Math Refresher

Making and Interpreting Graphs

Circle Graph

A circle graph, or pie chart, shows how each group of data relates to all of the data. Each part of the circle represents a category of the data. The entire circle represents all of the data. For example, a biologist studying a hardwood forest in Wisconsin found that there were five different types of trees. The data table at right summarizes the biologist's findings.

Wisconsin Hardwood Trees	
Type of tree	**Number found**
Oak	600
Maple	750
Beech	300
Birch	1,200
Hickory	150
Total	3,000

How to Make a Circle Graph

1 To make a circle graph of these data, first find the percentage of each type of tree. Divide the number of trees of each type by the total number of trees, and multiply by 100%.

$$\frac{600 \text{ oak}}{3,000 \text{ trees}} \times 100\% = 20\%$$

$$\frac{750 \text{ maple}}{3,000 \text{ trees}} \times 100\% = 25\%$$

$$\frac{300 \text{ beech}}{3,000 \text{ trees}} \times 100\% = 10\%$$

$$\frac{1,200 \text{ birch}}{3,000 \text{ trees}} \times 100\% = 40\%$$

$$\frac{150 \text{ hickory}}{3,000 \text{ trees}} \times 100\% = 5\%$$

A Community of Wisconsin Hardwood Trees

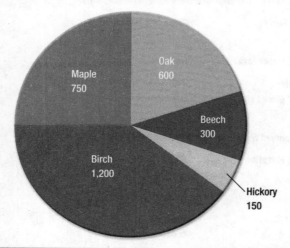

2 Now, determine the size of the wedges that make up the graph. Multiply each percentage by 360°. Remember that a circle contains 360°.

$$20\% \times 360° = 72° \qquad 25\% \times 360° = 90°$$

$$10\% \times 360° = 36° \qquad 40\% \times 360° = 144°$$

$$5\% \times 360° = 18°$$

3 Check that the sum of the percentages is 100 and the sum of the degrees is 360.

$$20\% + 25\% + 10\% + 40\% + 5\% = 100\%$$

$$72° + 90° + 36° + 144° + 18° = 360°$$

4 Use a compass to draw a circle and mark the center of the circle.

5 Then, use a protractor to draw angles of 72°, 90°, 36°, 144°, and 18° in the circle.

6 Finally, label each part of the graph, and choose an appropriate title.

Line Graphs

Line graphs are most often used to demonstrate continuous change. For example, Mr. Smith's students analyzed the population records for their hometown, Appleton, between 1910 and 2010. Examine the data at right.

Because the year and the population change, they are the variables. The population is determined by, or dependent on, the year. Therefore, the population is called the **dependent variable,** and the year is called the **independent variable**. Each year and its population make a **data pair**. To prepare a line graph, you must first organize data pairs into a table like the one at right.

Population of Appleton, 1910–2010	
Year	**Population**
1910	1,800
1930	2,500
1950	3,200
1970	3,900
1990	4,600
2010	5,300

How to Make a Line Graph

1 Place the independent variable along the horizontal (x) axis. Place the dependent variable along the vertical (y) axis.

2 Label the x-axis "Year" and the y-axis "Population." Look at your greatest and least values for the population. For the y-axis, determine a scale that will provide enough space to show these values. You must use the same scale for the entire length of the axis. Next, find an appropriate scale for the x-axis.

3 Choose reasonable starting points for each axis.

4 Plot the data pairs as accurately as possible.

5 Choose a title that accurately represents the data.

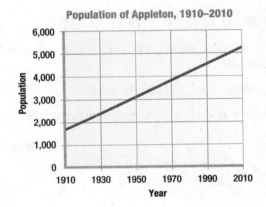

How to Determine Slope

Slope is the ratio of the change in the y-value to the change in the x-value, or "rise over run."

1 Choose two points on the line graph. For example, the population of Appleton in 2010 was 5,300 people. Therefore, you can define point A as (2010, 5,300). In 1910, the population was 1,800 people. You can define point B as (1910, 1,800).

2 Find the change in the y-value.
(y at point A) − (y at point B) = 5,300 people − 1,800 people = 3,500 people

3 Find the change in the x-value.
(x at point A) − (x at point B) = 2010 − 1910 = 100 years

4 Calculate the slope of the graph by dividing the change in y by the change in x.

$$slope = \frac{change\ in\ y}{change\ in\ x}$$

$$slope = \frac{3,500\ people}{100\ years}$$

$$slope = 35\ people\ per\ year$$

In this example, the population in Appleton increased by a fixed amount each year. The graph of these data is a straight line. Therefore, the relationship is **linear**. When the graph of a set of data is not a straight line, the relationship is **nonlinear**.

Math Refresher

Bar Graphs

Bar graphs can be used to demonstrate change that is not continuous. These graphs can be used to indicate trends when the data cover a long period of time. A meteorologist gathered the precipitation data shown here for Summerville for April 1–15 and used a bar graph to represent the data.

Precipitation in Summerville, April 1–15			
Date	Precipitation (cm)	Date	Precipitation (cm)
April 1	0.5	April 9	0.25
April 2	1.25	April 10	0.0
April 3	0.0	April 11	1.0
April 4	0.0	April 12	0.0
April 5	0.0	April 13	0.25
April 6	0.0	April 14	0.0
April 7	0.0	April 15	6.50
April 8	1.75		

How to Make a Bar Graph

1 Use an appropriate scale and a reasonable starting point for each axis.

2 Label the axes, and plot the data.

3 Choose a title that accurately represents the data.

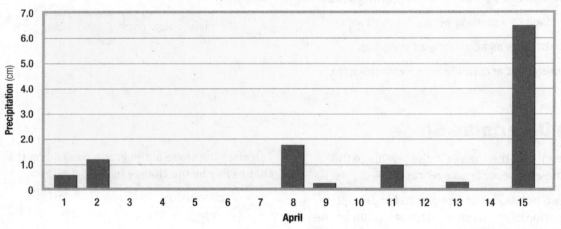

Precipitation in Summerville, April 1–15

Glossary

Pronunciation Key							
Sound	**Symbol**	**Example**	**Respelling**	**Sound**	**Symbol**	**Example**	**Respelling**
ă	a	pat	PAT	ŏ	ah	bottle	BAHT'l
ā	ay	pay	PAY	ō	oh	toe	TOH
âr	air	care	KAIR	ô	aw	caught	KAWT
ä	ah	father	FAH•ther	ôr	ohr	roar	ROHR
är	ar	argue	AR•gyoo	oi	oy	noisy	NOYZ•ee
ch	ch	chase	CHAYS	ŏŏ	u	book	BUK
ĕ	e	pet	PET	ōō	oo	boot	BOOT
ĕ (at end of a syllable)	eh	settee lessee	seh•TEE leh•SEE	ou	ow	pound	POWND
ĕr	ehr	merry	MEHR•ee	s	s	center	SEN•ter
ē	ee	beach	BEECH	sh	sh	cache	CASH
g	g	gas	GAS	ŭ	uh	flood	FLUHD
ĭ	i	pit	PIT	ûr	er	bird	BERD
ĭ (at end of a syllable)	ih	guitar	gih•TAR	z	z	xylophone	ZY•luh•fohn
ī	y eye (only for a complete syllable)	pie island	PY EYE•luhnd	z	z	bags	BAGZ
				zh	zh	decision	dih•SIZH•uhn
				ə	uh	around broken focus	uh•ROWND BROH•kuhn FOH•kuhs
îr	ir	hear	HIR	ər	er	winner	WIN•er
j	j	germ	JERM	th	th	thin they	THIN THAY
k	k	kick	KIK				
ng	ng	thing	THING	w	w	one	WUHN
ngk	ngk	bank	BANGK	wh	hw	whether	HWETH•er

alveolus (al·VEE·uh·luhs) tiny, thin-walled, capillary-rich sac in the lungs where the exchange of oxygen and carbon dioxide takes place; also called air sac (40)
　　alveolo saco diminuto ubicado en los pulmones, de paredes delgadas y rico en capilares, en donde ocurre el intercambio de oxígeno y dióxido de carbono

antibiotic (an·tih·by·AHT·ik) medicine used to kill bacteria and other microorganisms (120)
　　antibiótico medicina utilizada para matar bacterias y otros microorganismos

antibody (AN·tih·bahd·ee) a protein made by B cells that binds to a specific antigen (104)
　　anticuerpo una proteína producida por las células B que se une a un antígeno específico

antiviral drug (an·tee·VY·ruhl DRUHG) a drug that destroys viruses or prevents their growth or replication (120)
　　medicamento antiviral un medicamento que destruye a los virus o que evita que crezcan o se reproduzcan

artery (AR·tuh·ree) a blood vessel that carries blood away from the heart to the body's organs (35)
　　arteria un vaso sanguíneo que transporta sangre del corazón a los órganos del cuerpo

axon (AK·sahn) an elongated extension of a neuron that carries impulses away from the cell body (63)
　　axón una extensión alargada de una neurona que transporta impulsos hacia fuera del cuerpo de la célula

B cell (BEE SEL) a white blood cell that makes antibodies (104)
　　célula B un glóbulo blanco de la sangre que fabrica anticuerpos

blood (BLUHD) the fluid that carries gases, nutrients, and wastes through the body and that is made up of platelets, white blood cells, red blood cells, and plasma (30)
　　sangre el líquido que lleva gases, nutrientes y desechos por el cuerpo y que está formado por plaquetas, glóbulos blancos, glóbulos rojos y plasma

brain (BRAYN) the organ that is the main control center of the nervous system (60)
　　encéfalo el órgano que es el centro principal de control del sistema nervioso

bronchus (BRAHNG·kuhs) one of the two main branches of the trachea that lead directly to the lungs—plural, bronchii (40)
　　bronquio una de las dos ramificaciones principales de la tráquea que conducen directamente a los pulmones

capillary (KAP·uh·lehr·ee) a tiny blood vessel that allows an exchange between blood and cells in tissue (35)
　　capilar diminuto vaso sanguíneo que permite el intercambio entre la sangre y las células de los tejidos

cardiovascular system (kahr·dee·oh·VAS·kyuh·ler SIS·tuhm) a collection of organs that transport blood throughout the body; the organs in this system include the heart, the arteries, and the veins (30)
　　aparato cardiovascular un conjunto de órganos que transportan la sangre a través del cuerpo; los órganos de este sistema incluyen al corazón, las arterias y las venas

D

dendrite (DEN·dryt) branchlike extension of a neuron that receives impulses from neighboring neurons (63)
　　dendrita la extensión ramificada de una neurona que recibe impulsos de las neuronas vecinas

diet (DY·it) the type and amount of food that a person eats (128)
　　dieta el tipo y cantidad de alimento que come una persona

digestive system (dy·JES·tiv SIS·tuhm) the organs that break down food so that it can be used by the body (48)
　　aparato digestivo los órganos que descomponen la comida de modo que el cuerpo la pueda usar

E

eating disorder (EET·ing dis·OHR·der) a disease in which a person has an unhealthy concern for his or her body weight and shape (131)
　　trastorno alimenticio enfermedad en la que una persona se preocupa de manera negativa por su silueta y su peso corporal

egg (EG) a sex cell produced by a female (79)
　　óvulo una célula sexual producida por una hembra

embryo (EM·bree·oh) in humans, a developing individual from first division after fertilization through the 10th week of pregnancy (81)
　　embrión en los seres humanos, un individuo en desarrollo desde la primera división después de la fecundación hasta el final de la décima semana de embarazo

endocrine system (EN·duh·krin SIS·tuhm) a collection of glands and groups of cells that secrete hormones that regulate growth, development, and homeostasis; includes the pituitary, thyroid, parathyroid, and adrenal glands, the hypothalamus, the pineal body, and the gonads (66)
sistema endocrino un conjunto de glándulas y grupos de células que secretan hormonas las cuales regulan el crecimiento, desarrollo y homeostasis; incluye las glándulas pituitaria, tiroides, paratiroides y suprarrenal, el hipotálamo, el cuerpo pineal, y las gónadas

enzyme (EN·zym) a type of protein that speeds up metabolic reactions in plants and animals without being permanently changed or destroyed (49)
enzima un tipo de proteína que acelera las reacciones metabólicas en las plantas y animales, sin ser modificada permanentemente ni ser destruida

esophagus (ih·SAHF·uh·guhs) a long, straight tube that connects the pharynx to the stomach (50)
esófago un conducto largo y recto que conecta la faringe con el estómago

excretory system (EK·skrih·tohr·ee SIS·tuhm) the system that collects and excretes nitrogenous wastes and excess water from the body in the form of urine (53)
aparato excretor el sistema que recolecta y elimina del cuerpo los desperdicios nitrogenados y el exceso de agua en forma de orina

fetus (FEE·tuhs) a developing human from the end of the 10th week of pregnancy until birth (82)
feto un ser humano en desarrollo desde el final de la décima semana del embarazo hasta el nacimiento

gland (GLAND) a group of cells that make chemicals for use elsewhere in the body (66)
glándula un grupo de células que elaboran sustancias químicas para su utilización en otra parte del cuerpo

homeostasis (hoh·mee·oh·STAY·sis) the maintenance of a constant internal state in a changing environment (10)
homeostasis la capacidad de mantener un estado interno constante en un ambiente en cambio

hormone (HOHR·mohn) a substance that is made in one cell or tissue and that causes a change in another cell or tissue in a different part of the body (66)
hormona una sustancia que es producida en una célula o tejido, la cual causa un cambio en otra célula o tejido ubicado en una parte diferente del cuerpo

immune system (ih·MYOON SIS·tuhm) the cells and tissues that recognize and attack foreign substances in the body (103)
sistema inmunológico las células y tejidos que reconocen y atacan sustancias extrañas en el cuerpo

immunity (ih·MYOO·nih·tee) the ability to resist or recover from an infectious disease (106)
inmunidad la capacidad de resistir una enfermedad infecciosa o recuperarse de ella

infectious disease (in·FEK·shuhs dih·ZEEZ) a disease that is caused by a pathogen and that can be spread from one individual to another (115)
enfermedad infecciosa una enfermedad que es causada por un patógeno y que puede transmitirse de un individuo a otro

joint (JOYNT) a place where two or more bones meet (20)
articulación un lugar donde se unen dos o más huesos

kidney (KID·nee) one of the organs that filter water and wastes from the blood, excrete products as urine, and regulate the concentration of certain substances in the blood (54)
riñón uno de los órganos que filtran el agua y los desechos de la sangre, excretan productos como orina, y regulan la concentración de ciertas sustancias en la sangre

large intestine (LAHRJ in·TES·tin) the broader and shorter portion of the intestine, where water is removed from the mostly digested food to turn the waste into semisolid feces, or stool (51)
intestino grueso la porción más ancha y más corta del intestino, donde el agua se elimina de la mayoría de los alimentos digeridos para convertir los desechos en heces semisólidas o excremento

larynx (LAIR·ingks) the part of the respiratory system between the pharynx and the trachea; has walls of cartilage and muscle and contains the vocal cords (40)
laringe la parte del aparato respiratorio que se encuentra entre la faringe y la tráquea; tiene paredes de cartílago y músculo y contiene las cuerdas vocales

ligament (LIG·uh·muhnt) a type of tissue that holds together the bones in a joint (18)
ligamento un tipo de tejido que mantiene unidos los huesos en una articulación

liver (LIV·er) the largest organ in the body; it makes bile, stores and filters blood, and stores excess sugars as glycogen (52)

hígado el órgano más grande del cuerpo; produce bilis, almacena y filtra la sangre, y almacena el exceso de azúcares en forma de glucógeno

lymph (LIMF) the clear, watery fluid that leaks from blood vessels and contains white blood cells; circulates in lymphatic system; returned to bloodstream through lymph vessels (30)

linfa el fluido claro y acuoso que se filtra de los vasos sanguíneos y contiene glóbulos blancos; circula por el sistema linfático, regresa al torrente sanguíneo a través de los vasos linfáticos

lymph node (LIMF NOHD) small, bean-shaped masses of tissue that remove pathogens and dead cells from the lymph; concentrated in the armpits, neck, and groin; high concentration of white blood cells found in lymph nodes (32)

nodo linfático masas de tejido pequeñas y con forma de frijol que eliminan los patógenos y las células muertas de la linfa; están concentrados en las axilas, el cuello y la ingle; los nodos linfáticos presentan una alta concentración de glóbulos blancos

lymphatic system (lim·FAT·ik SIS·tuhm) a network of organs and tissues that collect the fluid that leaks from blood and returns it to blood vessels; includes lymph nodes, lymph vessels, and lymph; the place where certain white blood cells mature (30)

sistema linfático una red de órganos y tejidos que recolectan el fluido que se filtra de la sangre y lo regresan a los vasos sanguíneos; incluye los nodos linfáticos, los vasos linfáticos, y la linfa; el lugar donde maduran ciertos glóbulos blancos

macrophage (MAK·ruh·fayj) an immune system cell that engulfs pathogens and other materials (104)

macrófago una célula del sistema inmunológico que envuelve a los patógenos y otros materiales

muscular system (MUS·kyuh·ler SIS·tuhm) the organ system whose primary function is movement and flexibility (22)

sistema muscular el sistema de órganos cuya función principal es permitir el movimiento y la flexibilidad

nephron (NEF·rahn) the unit in the kidney that filters blood (54)

nefrona la unidad del riñón que filtra la sangre

nervous system (NER·vuhs SIS·tuhm) the structures that control the actions and reactions of the body in response to stimuli from the environment; it is formed by billions of specialized nerve cells, called neurons (60)

sistema nervioso las estructuras que controlan las acciones y reacciones del cuerpo en respuesta a los estímulos del ambiente; está formado por miles de millones de células nerviosas especializadas, llamadas neuronas

neuron (NUR·ahn) a nerve cell that is specialized to receive and conduct electrical impulses (62)

neurona una célula nerviosa que está especializada en recibir y transmitir impulsos eléctricos

noninfectious disease (nahn·in·FEK·shuhs dih·ZEEZ) a disease that cannot spread from one individual to another (114)

enfermedad no infecciosa una enfermedad que no se contagia de una persona a otra

nutrient (NOO·tree·uhnt) a substance in food that provides energy or helps form body tissues and that is necessary for life and growth (126)

nutriente una sustancia de los alimentos que proporciona energía o ayuda a formar tejidos corporales y que es necesaria para la vida y el crecimiento

nutrition (noo·TRISH·uhn) the science or study of food and the ways in which the body uses food (126)

nutrición ciencia o estudio de los alimentos y la forma en que el cuerpo los utiliza

obesity (oh·BEE·sih·tee) the state of having a significant amount of excess body fat; the state of weighing more than 20 percent above one's recommended body weight (130)

obesidad estado en el que una persona tiene una cantidad significativa de grasa corporal en exceso; estado en el que el peso corporal de una persona supera en más de un 20 por ciento su peso corporal recomendado

ovary (OH·vuh·ree) in the female reproductive system of animals, an organ that produces eggs (79)

ovario en el aparato reproductor femenino de los animales, un órgano que produce óvulos

overweight (oh·ver·WAYT) heavy for one's height (130)

sobrepeso excedido de peso en relación a su estatura

pancreas (PANG·kree·uhs) the organ that lies behind the stomach and that makes digestive enzymes and hormones that regulate sugar levels (52)
páncreas el órgano que se encuentra detrás del estómago y que produce las enzimas digestivas y las hormonas que regulan los niveles de azúcar

pathogen (PATH·uh·juhn) a microorganism, another organism, a virus, or a protein that causes disease (102)
patógeno un microorganismo, otro organismo, un virus o una proteína que causa enfermedades

penis (PEE·nis) the male organ that transfers sperm to a female and that carries urine out of the body (78)
pene el órgano masculino que transfiere espermatozoides a una hembra y que lleva la orina hacia el exterior del cuerpo

pharynx (FAIR·ingks) the part of the respiratory system that extends from the mouth to the larynx (40)
faringe la parte del aparato respiratorio que va de la boca a la laringe

physical fitness (FIZ·ih·kuhl FIT·nis) the ability to perform daily physical activities without becoming short of breath, sore, or overly tired (132)
buen estado físico capacidad de realizar actividades físicas todos los días sin sentir falta de aire, dolor o cansancio extremos

placenta (pluh·SEN·tuh) the partly fetal and partly maternal organ by which materials are exchanged between a fetus and the mother (82)
placenta el órgano parcialmente fetal y parcialmente materno por medio del cual se intercambian materiales entre el feto y la madre

R

respiratory system (RES·per·uh·tohr·ee SIS·tuhm) a collection of organs whose primary function is to take in oxygen and expel carbon dioxide; the organs of this system include the lungs, the throat, and the passageways that lead to the lungs (39)
aparato respiratorio un conjunto de órganos cuya función principal es tomar oxígeno y expulsar dióxido de carbono; los órganos de este aparato incluyen a los pulmones, la garganta, y las vías que llevan a los pulmones

skeletal system (SKEL·ih·tl SIS·tuhm) the organ system whose primary function is to support and protect the body and to allow the body to move (16)
sistema esquelético el sistema de órganos cuya función principal es sostener y proteger el cuerpo y permitir que se mueva

small intestine (SMAWL in·TES·tin) the organ between the stomach and the large intestine where most of the breakdown of food happens and most of the nutrients from food are absorbed (51)
intestino delgado el órgano que se encuentra entre el estómago y el intestino grueso en el cual se produce la mayor parte de la descomposición de los alimentos y se absorben la mayoría de los nutrientes

sperm (SPERM) the male sex cell (78)
espermatozoide la célula sexual masculina

spinal cord (SPY·nuhl KOHRD) a column of nerve tissue running from the base of the brain through the vertebral column (60)
médula espinal una columna de tejido nervioso que se origina en la base del cerebro y corre a lo largo de la columna vertebral

stomach (STUHM·uhk) the saclike, digestive organ that is between the esophagus and the small intestine and that breaks down food by the action of muscles, enzymes, and acids (51)
estómago el órgano digestivo con forma de bolsa, ubicado entre el esófago y el intestino delgado, que descompone la comida por la acción de músculos, enzimas, y ácidos

T cell (TEE SEL) an immune system cell that coordinates the immune system and attacks many infected cells (104)
célula T una célula del sistema inmunológico que coordina el sistema inmunológico y ataca a muchas células infectadas

tendon (TEN·duhn) a tough connective tissue that attaches a muscle to a bone or to another body part (23)
tendón un tejido conectivo duro que une un músculo con un hueso o con otra parte del cuerpo

testes (TES·teez) the primary male reproductive organs, which produce sperm cells and testosterone (singular, testis) (78)
testículos los principales órganos reproductores masculinos, los cuales producen espermatozoides y testosterona

trachea (TRAY·kee·uh) thin-walled tube that extends from the larynx to the bronchi; carries air to the lungs; also called windpipe (40)
tráquea el conducto de paredes delgadas que va de la laringe a los bronquios; lleva el aire a los pulmones

umbilical cord (uhm·BIL·ih·kuhl KOHRD) the ropelike structure through which blood vessels pass and by which a developing mammal is connected to the placenta (82)

cordón umbilical la estructura con forma de cuerda a través de la cual pasan vasos sanguíneos y por medio de la cual un mamífero en desarrollo está unido a la placenta

urine (YUR·in) the liquid excreted by the kidneys, stored in the bladder, and passed through the urethra to the outside of the body (54)

orina el líquido que excretan los riñones, se almacena en la vejiga, y pasa a través de la uretra hacia el exterior del cuerpo

uterus (YOO·ter·uhs) in female placental mammals, the hollow, muscular organ in which an embryo embeds itself and develops into a fetus (80)

útero en los mamíferos placentarios hembras, el órgano hueco y muscular en el que el embrión se incrusta y se desarrolla hasta convertirse en feto

V–Z

vaccine (vak·SEEN) a substance that is prepared from killed or weakened pathogens or from genetic material and that is introduced into a body to produce immunity (106)

vacuna una sustancia que se prepara a partir de organismos patógenos muertos o debilitados o a partir de material genético y que se introduce en el cuerpo para producir inmunidad

vagina (vuh·JY·nuh) the female reproductive organ that connects the outside of the body to the uterus (80)

vagina el órgano reproductivo femenino que conecta la parte exterior del cuerpo con el útero

vein (VAYN) in biology, a vessel that carries blood to the heart (35)

vena en biología, un vaso que lleva sangre al corazón

Index

Page numbers for definitions are printed in **boldface** type.
Page numbers for illustrations, maps, and charts are printed in *italics*.